Contents

Summary

In August 2004 the world's athletes will gather in Athens for the Summer Olympic Games. New records will be set. Contestants will run faster, jump higher, and throw farther than ever before – and global sportswear firms will spend vast sums of money to associate their products with the Olympian ideal. Images of Olympic events, complete with corporate branding, will be televised to a global audience.

This report looks behind the branding to ask fundamental questions about the global sportswear industry – questions that go to the heart of debates on poverty, workers' rights, trade, and globalisation. *'Olympism,'* in the words of the Olympic Charter, *'seeks to create a way of life based on the joy found in effort, the educational value of good example, and respect for universal fundamental ethical principles.'* We show that the business practices of major sportswear companies violate both the spirit and the letter of the Charter. Corporate profits in this industry are created at the expense of the dignity, health, and safety of vulnerable men and women, contravening universal ethical principles. Yet the Olympics movement, particularly the International Olympics Committee, has been remarkably silent in the face of these contraventions.

The expansion of international trade in sportswear goods under the auspices of corporate giants such as Nike, Adidas, Reebok, Puma, Fila, ASICS, Mizuno, Lotto, Kappa, and Umbro has drawn millions of people, mainly women, into employment. From China and Indonesia to Turkey and Bulgaria, these workers are cutting, stitching, assembling and packaging the goods that will be sold through retail chains worldwide. Far away from the media spotlight that will fall on the Athens Olympic Stadium, they are involved in an epic struggle of their own – a struggle for survival. They are working long hours for low wages in arduous conditions, often without the most basic employment protection. The rights to join and form trade unions and to engage in collective bargaining are systematically violated.

If labour exploitation were an Olympic sport, the sportswear giants would be well represented among the medal winners. While the industry can boast its commitment to some impressive principles, enshrined in codes of conduct, its business practices generate the market pressures that are in reality leading to exploitative labour conditions. The consequence is that millions of workers are being locked into poverty and denied a fair share of the wealth that they generate. The sportswear industry is reinforcing a pattern of globalisation that produces insecurity and vulnerability for the many – alongside prosperity for the few.

The business model that drives globalisation is at the centre of the problem. This model is based upon ruthless pressure on prices, a demand for fast and flexible delivery, and a constant shift in manufacturing locations in pursuance of ever-cheaper production costs. Global sportswear companies link millions of workers to consumer markets via long supply-chains and complex networks of factories and contractors. Market power enables global companies to demand that their suppliers cut prices, shorten delivery times, and adjust rapidly to fluctuating orders. Inevitably, the resulting pressures are transmitted down the supply-chain to workers, leading to lower wages, bad conditions, and the violation of workers' rights.

For many of these workers, the ability to defend themselves from exploitation and abuse is thwarted by the repression of their rights to form and join trade unions and to bargain collectively. Too many obstacles – be they administrative or legal, or lack of an identifiable or legitimate employer because of the complexity of these supply-chains, or sheer fear through intimidation and harassment – still exist, leaving them exposed and vulnerable to unfair, inhumane, and undignified treatment by employers.

Chapter 1

of this report documents the harsh reality of life for those working at the bottom of the global supply-chain. It does so on the basis of evidence collected in interviews with 186 workers from six different countries – Bulgaria, Cambodia, China, Indonesia, Thailand, and Turkey. The interviews reveal a pattern of abysmally low wages, workers being forced to work excessively long hours, exploitative terms of employment, bullying, sexual harassment, and physical and verbal abuse. Involvement in trade union activity is effectively outlawed. Some of the most insidious violations of workers' rights revealed by our research include the following:

► Indonesian workers attacked, intimidated, and harassed for participating in union activities;

► Bulgarian workers fined or fired for refusing to do overtime work;

► workers in all these countries sewing sportswear for up to 16 hours a day, six days a week, especially during peak seasons; and

► Chinese workers receiving wages as low as US$ 12 per month during the low season.

Chapter 2

considers the global market for sportswear goods – a market which generated US$ 58 billion in 2002. Increasing competition has led to an intense squeeze on prices, as companies seek to expand their market-share through ruthless price competition: the average price of a pair of trainers in the USA has fallen from US$ 41 to US $36 since 1997. Suppliers have been left in a market characterised by falling unit prices, juxtaposed with rising production costs. For example, a Honduran supplier of sportswear to global companies reported a fall of 23 per cent in unit prices over three years. Inevitably, the workers at the very end of the supply-chain bear the brunt of this price squeeze, as factory managers work them harder, to produce more, in a shorter time, and for less money.

Along with the price squeeze, suppliers have been forced to adjust to wider pressures. The traditional system of ordering in bulk has been replaced by a system in which factories are now required to supply smaller amounts on the basis of monthly and even weekly orders. Lead-times have been shortened. Adidas, for instance, aims to reduce its lead-times for athletic apparel from 120 to 90 days. On the factory floor, this is translating into excessive working hours and forced overtime in the rush to complete orders in time for export.

Global sportswear companies are careful to distance themselves from accusations that their business operations – the way in which they place orders and negotiate price cuts – are having negative consequences in the workplace. They point to statements of corporate social responsibility and codes of conduct covering labour practices as evidence of their good intent. As we show in this report, this defence is tenuous. The industry's business model creates clear market signals to suppliers, placing a premium on the creation of low-wage, temporary workforces, denied basic workers' rights.

Supporting this business model, governments eager to attract foreign investors to their shores erode workers' rights in order to offer a cheaper, more flexible workforce. The right to join a trade union and bargain collectively is often the first right to be denied, leaving workers unprotected and vulnerable to exploitation and abuse.

Chapter 3

suggests why significant improvements to working conditions within the supply-chains of major sportswear companies have not been achieved. Despite extensive world-wide public campaigning which has contributed in part to the numerous ethical commitments and codes of conduct on labour practices, too little progress has been made. The report highlights three major reasons for this:

Corporate practices do not match ethical policies.

The ethical commitments made by purchasing companies are contradicted by their aggressive purchasing practices. Corporate staff responsible for sourcing and ordering goods are often unaware of (or indifferent to) the impact on workers of their demands for lower prices and shorter delivery times, and the constant threat of relocation. Having to choose between retaining their customers and protecting workers' rights, factory managers inevitably opt for the former. In their search for low prices and quick turnaround times, companies regularly shift from one supplier to another, favouring such short term rather than long term relationships with suppliers. The implied threat of relocation and the associated loss of jobs mean that corporate purchasing practices also have a negative impact on workers.

Compliance models are flawed.

Some companies are simply not genuine in their commitments to respect labour standards. Our research reveals a number of companies which have adopted comprehensive codes of labour practices in principle but do little to put them into practice. Some companies have not demonstrated any effective implementation of their codes in the workplace. Evidence reveals that some factory managers simply falsify the evidence during social audits and carry on with business as usual once the inspectors have left. The fact that workers are not adequately involved in the current compliance processes has meant that few substantive or sustainable improvements have been made.

Bad practices by one company undermine the good practices of others.

Many sports-brands tend to share the same suppliers. As suppliers face tremendous pressure from this cut-throat industry to reduce prices, shorten lead-times, and make the workforce more flexible, the influence of the few sportswear

The goal of Olympism is to place everywhere sport at the service of the harmonious development of man, with a view to encouraging the establishment of a peaceful society concerned with the preservation of human dignity

"The Olympics Charter"

companies that do ask for labour standards to be respected in the workplace is marginalised by the many who place little importance upon these standards in the normal run of the business.

Play fair at the Olympics

In launching this report and the **Play Fair at the Olympics Campaign**, the Clean Clothes Campaign network, Oxfam, and Global Unions[1] are lending support to the continued struggle of a worldwide movement led by workers, trade unions, and non-government organisations, along with concerned citizens. In choosing to draw attention to this issue in advance of the Olympic Games in Athens in 2004, we hope that the Olympic movement will reaffirm its pledge to preserve human dignity by calling upon the sportswear industry to make trade fair by ensuring decent, just, and dignified conditions for workers employed in its supply-chains.

This report argues that the Olympic movement has the power to ensure that the sportswear industry improves employment conditions and standards for millions of workers. Apart from asserting the moral imperative, the International Olympics Committee (IOC), as the primary holder of the rights to use the Olympics logo, and as the protector of the Olympics brand, can and should enforce changes by building into licensing and sponsorship contracts commitments to respect labour standards. The movement should be using its influence to ensure that workers in the sportswear industry are employed under fair, dignified, and safe conditions.

While the report provides evidence of the ways in which the operations of a number of companies in the sportswear industry are having a negative impact on working conditions, public campaigning for Play Fair at the Olympics will focus upon the IOC and selected companies who – given the size of their market share and popularity with consumers – need to do much more to meet their responsibilities towards workers in their supply-chain. These sportswear companies include **ASICS Corporation,** a publicly owned Japanese company; **Fila,** a privately owned US company; **Kappa** and **Lotto,** both publicly owned Italian companies; **Mizuno,** a publicly owned Japanese company; **Puma,** a publicly owned German company; and **Umbro,** a privately owned British company.

Recommendations for change

▶ **Sportswear companies** should develop and implement credible labour-practice policies which ensure that their suppliers respect internationally recognised labour standards, including the right to a living wage based on a regular working week that does not exceed 48 hours; humane working hours with no forced overtime; a safe and healthy workplace free from harassment; and legal employment, with labour and social protection.

▶ **Sportswear companies** should change their purchasing practices to ensure that they do not lead to the exploitation of workers. They should negotiate appropriate delivery times, as well as fair prices which allow factory managers to meet orders *and* meet labour standards.

▶ **Sportswear companies** should implement their codes of conduct on labour practices in ways that deliver sustainable improvements to working conditions. This requires communicating in clear terms to their suppliers – factory managers and their sub-contractors – that respect for the rights to join and form trade unions and to engage in collective bargaining are of paramount importance if working conditions are to be improved, and that undermining these rights is unacceptable. Further requirements are investment in appropriate inspection systems which place workers at the centre of the process; increased training for workers on their rights and related issues; and ensuring safe complaint mechanisms.

▶ **The sportswear industry** should make the effort to address these problems collectively, given that they are endemic in the industry, by jointly developing a sector-wide approach with trade unions and NGOs for a programme of work that promotes the organisation of workers in trade unions, overcomes the limits of the current ethical policies of companies, and ensures on-going dialogue between companies in this sector and the International Textile, Garment and Leather Workers Federation, the representative organisation of workers in the sportswear industry at global level, via a sectoral framework agreement.

▶ **Sportswear companies** should commit themselves to be transparent about – and publicly accountable for – the impact of their business operations on workers.

▶ **Sportswear suppliers** should provide decent jobs for their employees by complying with international labour standards and national labour laws.

In particular, they should ensure that workers are allowed to exercise their rights to join trade unions and bargain collectively.

► **Governments** should stop trading away workers' rights in law and in practice, and should enforce national laws and international labour standards in order to guarantee decent employment for all their workers.

► **The Olympics movement** should make a serious commitment to respect workers' rights in the sportswear industry. Through the International Olympics Committee (IOC), the National Olympics Committees (NOC), and the Organising Committees (OCOGs) it should be insisting that the industry must meet international labour standards in its operations. The **IOC** should make a public commitment to this in its charter and should reform its rules on licensing, sponsorship, and marketing agreements to ensure that commitments on workers' rights are included in these contracts.

► **The public** should insist that sportswear companies adopt clear commitments to make sure that internationally recognised labour standards are respected throughout their supply-chains; demand that their purchasing practices support rather than undermine workers' rights; and demand that they are transparent about their policies on (and implementation of) labour practices and the impacts on working conditions.

Join the Play Fair at the Olympics campaign at www.fairolympics.org

Introduction

In 490 BC, Phidippides, the most celebrated runner in antiquity, arrived in Athens at the end of his final race. He was carrying news of a great Athenian victory in the face of overwhelming odds against Persian forces on the plain of Marathon, 42 km away. Legend tells that Phidippides arrived in Athens and with his last breath uttered the word *'Nike'* – the name of the Greek goddess of victory – before he collapsed and died. His achievement inspired one of the showpiece events of the modern Olympic games.

During the summer of 2004, the image of Phidippides will figure prominently in the marketing of the twenty-eighth Olympic games, which will be held in Athens. As the games draw closer, the finest athletes in the world are preparing themselves for the effort of a lifetime. Many will set new world records. They will run faster, throw farther, and leap higher than ever before. And, as the contests are fought and the medals are distributed, the corporate gods of the modern Olympics will be in close attendance. Nike, along with Adidas, Reebok, Fila, Puma, ASICS, and Mizuno, are investing billions of dollars in advertising and branding for the Olympics. For these corporate giants of the sportswear industry, the Athens games provide an opportunity to expand profits and build markets through an association with sporting success and the Olympian ideal.

While the world's media spend two weeks focusing on the struggle for sporting success, away from the cameras thousands of workers – mostly women in the developing world – employed to produce the tracksuits, trainers, vests, and team uniforms will be engaged in a different type of struggle. They too are breaking records for the global sportswear industry: working ever-faster for ever-longer periods of time under arduous conditions for poverty-level wages, to produce more goods and more profit. Yet for them there are no medals, rewards, or recognition from the industry that they service.

The sportswear industry often responds to evidence of exploitative labour practices by reciting familiar arguments about the need to recognise 'market realities'. Low wages, it claims, are a product of poverty, not of corporate malpractice. When it comes to attributing responsibility, many of the global firms highlighted in this report blame governments and local suppliers, absolving themselves of responsibility. They cite their own codes of conduct on labour practice as evidence of their good intent.

Yet what our report shows is that these statements of good intent are at variance with the practices of the business model used by these global companies. This is a model that is creating huge disincentives to protect workers' rights. Facing intense price competition at the retail end, global sportswear companies place demands on their suppliers to reduce their prices, speed up the manufacturing process, and meet their demands for flexible production and delivery. In response, suppliers transfer the costs down to their workers, making them work longer, faster, and cheaper. Further, the constant relocation by companies from supplier to supplier in search of the cheapest price creates peaks and troughs in demand for labour that lead to job insecurity and a reliance on flexible workforces, employed on short-term contracts. In short, the market conditions created by the new business models of the global sportswear industry are inconsistent with decent employment practices.

Global sportswear firms can no longer hide behind claims of non-accountability for exploitative working conditions in their supply-chains. As intermediaries between consumers in rich countries and producers in poor ones, the sportswear companies have responsibilities which go beyond the generation of profit and returns to shareholders. Over the past 15 years a powerful movement of organisations – including trade unions, human-rights activists, women's rights groups, migrant-labour organisations, and consumer groups – has emerged to challenge global corporations in the sportswear industry. That movement has vigorously campaigned for better terms of employment, lending support to workers' own struggles against sweatshop conditions worldwide. These campaigns have increased consumers' awareness of the links between the products bought in rich countries and the labour conditions prevailing in poor ones. They have also forced the issue of workers' rights on to the agendas of corporate boardrooms, governments, and international financial institutions. A recent ILO-commissioned report[2] concludes: *'Perhaps no issue is as critical to the sectors of apparel, footwear and retail goods production as is the sweatshop issue.'*

This report takes stock of what the sportswear industry has done to meet its responsibilities to workers in their supply-chains. It reveals that while some companies – particularly those that have been exposed to public campaigning – have made promising efforts to address the issues, others have either simply not bothered to deal with them or have made superficial attempts to placate the public through public-relations exercises. Drawing on evidence of exploitative and abusive working conditions in sportswear production sites from six countries, the report points to the failure of the industry as a whole to address the root causes of the problem. The report particularly documents the truly shameful record of those companies that have done little to meet their obligations. It concludes by suggesting what needs to be done to create the conditions under which the industry can support the development of globalisation with a human face.

In all, the research included interviews with 186 workers, nine factory managers and owners, and ten representatives of brand companies. We have changed the names of all the factory workers interviewed, in order to protect their identity, because many feared that they would lose their jobs for speaking out. We have also concealed the identity of most of the factories, to avoid jeopardising their business relationships with the companies that they supply, as well as to protect their workers from undue negative consequences. Those factories that have been revealed are those where the workers have been involved in public campaigning to improve working conditions in their workplace and have agreed to their factories being named. All interviews were conducted between May 2003 and January 2004: with Thai workers in May and June 2003; with Indonesian workers in October 2003; with Bulgarian workers between July and October 2003; with Chinese workers in November 2003; with Turkish workers between November 2003 and January 2004; and with Cambodian workers in December 2003. Factory managers were interviewed between October and December 2003. Representatives from brand companies were interviewed and communicated with between July 2003 and February 2004. All local currency amounts have been converted into US dollars, using exchange rates current in January 2004.

Many well-known brand companies feature in this report. Practices vary considerably from company to company. Where particular companies are linked to particular criticism (or indeed to specific good practice), we have made this clear. Generalised statements about industry practices should not, however, be taken to refer to any particular company.

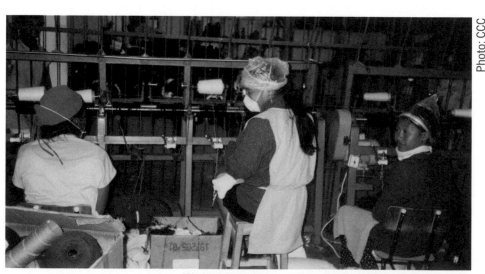

Working at the bottom of the global supply-chain in Cambodia

Chapter 1

Faster, Longer, Cheaper

Women working in a sportswear factory in Bulgaria

1: Faster, Longer, Cheaper

Phan, 22-year-old migrant worker, sews sportswear for Puma at garment factory S in Thailand. This is her account of life at the factory.

'Every day we work from 8 am until noon, then break for lunch. After lunch we work again from 1 pm until 5 pm. We have to do overtime every day, starting from 5.30 pm. We work until 2 am or 3 am during the peak season. We always have to work a double shift. Although we are very exhausted, we have no choice. We cannot refuse overtime work, because our standard wages are so low. Sometimes we want to rest, but our employer forces us to work.

'I earn around US$ 50 per month, but I pay US$ 3 for electricity, water, and dormitory. I also pay US$ 5 for rice. The employer also asks us to pay US$ 7 per month for the workers' registration fee. So, I only have US$ 35 left for all my other living expenses. In some months during the low season when I earn less, I only have 30 or 40 cents left[3] that month.

'I would like to demand the improvement of working conditions. However, we do not feel we can demand higher wages, welfare, and legal status.'

Phan's experience resonates with that of thousands of workers in the global sportswear industry. In interviews with workers in athletic apparel and footwear factories across seven countries, accounts of excessively long working hours, forced overtime, lack of job and wage security, poverty wages, denial of the right to unionise, poor health, exhaustion, mental stress, and dysfunctional family life were repeated over and over again. The reality of life in a sportswear factory, particularly in the workplace further down in the supply chain, is a far cry from the guaranteed workers' rights that are stipulated by law, or indeed the ethical commitments on labour standards proclaimed by many of the big global sports brands.

A sportswear factory in Madagascar

Too long and too hard

Long working hours and forced overtime are of most serious concern to all the women workers to whom we spoke. Factory managers typically push employees to work between 10 and 12 hours, sometimes extending to between 16 and 18 hours without a proper break. When order deadlines loom, working hours lengthen. A seven-day working week is becoming the norm during the peak season, particularly in China, despite limits being placed by the law. In two Chinese factories[4] producing for Umbro, workers said that they were made to work a seven-day week frequently during the peak season. In one factory they worked a total of 120 hours of overtime during the month of October 2003 – three times in excess of Chinese labour legislation. *'We have endless overtime in the peak season and we sit working non-stop for 13 to 14 hours a day. We sewing workers work like this every day – we sew and sew without stopping until our arms feel sore and stiff,'* said one of the workers. A 21-year-old woman working in sports garment factory H in Indonesia reported having to work more than 12 consecutive hours of overtime to meet an export deadline: *'In June and July 2003, the sewing department I am part of worked from 7 am until 4 am the next day because of a large Reebok order. We were allowed to go home for about seven hours, but had to be back at the factory at 11 am to work until 10 pm.'* Krishanti, a 28-year-old worker in Bangkok garment Factory T producing for Fila, Nike, and Puma, reports: *'Sometimes we had to work on overtime in a night shift. It upsets the normal body functioning ... I work like a machine, not a human being.'*

Overtime is usually compulsory; and workers are informed only at the last minute that they are expected to perform the extra hours. In four Turkish factories[5] producing for Lotto, Fila, Puma, and Kappa, workers all reported being forced to work overtime. In many instances, workers report being threatened with dismissal and subjected to penalties as well as verbal abuse if they cannot work the additional hours. Soy, a garment worker at a Cambodian sportswear factory,[6] told researchers: *'They force us to work overtime. If we refuse three times, the managers threaten us with dismissal. If we refuse to work on Sundays or public holidays, they also threaten us.'* In Bulgarian factory U supplying Puma, refusal to do overtime is often used as a pretext for dismissing the worker. Fines are imposed on those who do not work the overtime hours as instructed. In a Chinese factory Q, producing for Umbro, workers were fined RMB 30 (US$ 3.60) for refusal to work overtime. In extreme cases, workers in three factories in China – two producing for Umbro[7] and one for Mizuno and Kappa[8] – reported being prevented from resigning during peak production periods. The management does this by retaining their wages (ranging from half a month to two months' worth). Often, management do not pay workers the overtime premium rate as stipulated by law.

'In our factory overtime is compulsory. If you do not accept this, you cannot work here.'

(Garment worker in Factory X, which supplies Lotto)

For those with families, working days that often start in the early hours of the morning and extend late into the night leave little time for child-care or family life. Laila, who works in Indonesian factory D, producing goods for Fila, Puma, Lotto, Nike, Adidas, and ASICS, laments: *'There is no time for housework. For our friends who have children, we hear from them that they feel very upset in their hearts, that they never get time to spend with their children and to watch them grow. During the spare time we do have, we feel constantly exhausted.'* A fellow Indonesian worker from Factory I, producing goods bearing the logos of Umbro and Puma and the Olympics emblem, adds: *'When there are stretches of overtime work, many workers who have children never get to see them. When they come home from work, their children are already sleeping. And all of us have to come to work so early in the morning that the children are usually asleep in the morning too. Family life is cut short.'* As a worker in Bulgarian factory U sadly concludes: *'It is chaos at home.'*

BOX 1: The health costs of working in a sportswear factory

'I have many health problems: headaches, diarrhoea, stomach flu, back pains, and muscle cramps. All these are caused by the situation in the factory – the bad air, having to stand all day, and the long hours of work without sufficient rest, water or food.'
(Fatima, a 22-year-old Indonesian woman worker making products for Adidas, Fila, Nike, Puma, and Lotto in Factory D)

'Exhaustion is the main thing after overtime hours. Many women tend to miscarry pregnancies because of the continuous work that is caused by overtime work following immediately after the daily shift.'
(Ita, a 25-year-old worker making products for Umbro and Puma in Factory I)

At a Bulgarian factory producing exclusively for Puma, workers spoke of eye damage, varicose veins, back pain, dust allergies, respiratory diseases, and repetitive strain injuries.

Poverty wages

The wages of the many workers who sew, assemble, and pack sportswear for export are not enough to guarantee a decent existence for them and their families. Workers in Indonesian factory G, producing for Reebok, told researchers, *'We have many living costs here. We have rent to pay for the dorms; we have food and transport costs. We need at least Rp 10,000 (US$ 1.19) per day for food and transportation. The company gives us only Rp 2,000 (US$ 0.23) per day for transportation. If workers have children, the daily cost of living is at least Rp 25,000 (US$ 2.97). A wage which would allow us to live and make some savings every month would be at least 1 million rupiah (US$ 119).'* At the time of our research, the standard monthly take-home wage at this factory was only Rp 816,000 (US$ 98.6), 82 per cent of the amount needed.

Overtime work presents a dilemma. Workers universally hate it for the toll that it takes upon their health, their personal lives, and their family lives. Yet the extra payment (when it is made) brought in by overtime work can make the difference between starvation and subsistence wages. As one worker states: *'We need overtime work because our basic wages are not enough to meet all of our living needs. We have rent to pay for the dorms that we rent on a monthly basis, we have food and transport money that is needed.'*

Some of the workers interviewed asked themselves why they worked so hard for so little. Yet for many, the choice to leave is simply not available. As one garment worker from a Turkish factory[9] producing for Puma and Lotto said: *'The wages are so scant and not sufficient for anything. But we do not have any alternative because wages in garment factories are nearly all the same. Our choice is between this wage and unemployment.'*

Campaigning on working conditions in global supply-chains has persistently focused upon getting employers to pay workers a living wage: a wage that allows workers and their families to live in dignity. Such a wage would provide for basic needs – food, clothing, health care, housing, potable water, electricity, education, child care, transportation – and a discretionary income that would allow savings to be made. In many countries, the legal minimum wage – and many workers in the sportswear industry do not earn even this – does not amount to a living wage.

'We have overtime work until 11 pm or midnight everyday. The price they pay us per piece is so low, so there is no point to us working such long hours. If our income was higher, I would have no complaints. But all we have now is exhaustion and a low income. Some of us do not even have enough money to spend on food. It is more than we can bear.'

(Garment worker in Factory R, which supplies well-known sports-brands including Nike, Fila, Arena, Adidas, and Reebok)

Employed – but on precarious terms

Factories often do not issue workers with proper employment contracts, leaving workers no means of redress when their employers fail to respect labour laws on minimum wages, working hours, payment of overtime premiums, provision of health benefits and other forms of insurance, as well as other legal rights. This is further exacerbated when workers are denied their right to join and form trade unions. Many workers – especially migrants – do not feel able to ask for such contracts, and their absence has become accepted as an industry norm. Even where contracts are issued, employers still flout their terms and conditions. Jing, a worker in China-based sportswear factory N, producing for Mizuno and Kappa, told researchers: *'The contract is a scrap. The factory management never give us what is written in the contract. Talk about no overtime work for more than three hours? I can't remember having a day where I have worked for less than three overtime hours.'*

Among the worst-treated in the industry are workers who are employed on a temporary basis. Often, factories continually hire them on temporary contracts as a means of evading legal responsibilities to pay time-rate wages or benefits such as maternity leave, health insurance, or severance pay. Workers interviewed from a number of factories reported that, despite being employed by the same factory for periods as long as two years, they were still on temporary contracts. This sort of employment is a particular phenomenon in Indonesia. Another tactic is to hire workers from an agency, where the employer is the agency rather than the owner of the factory. Thus, the enterprise that owns the factory is able to avoid its obligations as an employer. Unions see this as a major barrier to organising workers. When interviewed, a number of union leaders reported that temporary workers who seek to join in union activities often find that their contracts are not renewed.

Many of the workers interviewed reported not receiving legal benefits such as health insurance or wage protection during periods of sick leave or maternity leave. This adds to the precarious nature of their employment. At one Cambodian garment factory,[10] producing for Adidas and Puma, if workers went on sick leave for three days, the employer deducted one day's salary; if more than three days of sick leave were taken, the employer made the worker sign a form allowing the factory to deduct the worker's incentive bonus for that month. At Indonesian Factory B, a worker reported that taking leave was at the expense of wage cuts and other penalties: *'We are not allowed to take sick leave...If we do anyway, when we come back to work our daily wages are also cut. I have experienced being moved to the cleaning department from the sewing department after I took sick leave. It was humiliating. If we don't agree to move departments, then we are forced to leave the factory without any severance pay or benefits.'* It is also common for workers to be denied proper severance pay when dismissed or made redundant.

BOX 2: Dignity returns – the case of the Bed & Bath workers

In October 2002, the owners of Bed & Bath Prestige, a Thai garment-manufacturing company, suddenly shut down their factory, leaving their workers in a desperate state. Prior to closure, the company produced for a number of global brands, including sportswear brands Adidas, Nike, Fila, and Umbro. The demands made on workers in the factory had been extreme. Interviewed in October and November 2002, workers reported that when orders had to be completed quickly, workers were provided with amphetamines to help them to work right through the night. It was later revealed that orders accepted by the company were also being sub-contracted to other factories, where working conditions were also very bad. Owing their workers approximately US$ 400,000 in unpaid wages and severance pay, the owners left for the USA. Unable to pursue the owners directly, 350 workers from the main Bed & Bath factory campaigned persistently for the Thai Ministry of Labour to pay

compensation for their illegal treatment. The workers also demanded that those companies who were former clients of Bed & Bath should contribute to paying workers what they were owed. Although some of the companies encouraged the Thai government to respond to workers' demands, they refused to accept that they themselves had a moral responsibility to ensure that the workers received their legal entitlements. Finally in January 2003, the Ministry agreed to pay the workers the equivalent of four months' wages. The workers also succeeded in persuading the Thai government to amend the law regarding severance pay, increasing the amount paid to workers employed for more than six years from 30 to 60 times the daily minimum wage. The workers have since established a co-operative, producing apparel under the name 'Solidarity Group', with their slogan '*Dignity Returns*'. They continue to campaign for their former employers to be brought to justice in Thailand.

Bullied, humiliated, abused

Managers in the factories often resort to harassment, humiliation, and abuse in order to exert their authority over the workers. Elina, a garment worker in Indonesian factory PT Busana Prima Global[11] making goods for Lotto, said: *'There is a lot of verbal abuse. The management calls us names throughout the time when we work. They call us "stupid", "lazy", "useless", "bastard's child", and other crass words. They say "You don't deserve any more than this". Some girls start crying. Physical abuse happens too. Our ears are often pulled, and managers yell directly into our ears.'* More disturbing are regular incidences of sexual harassment of young women workers at these factories. At Indonesian factory D, producing for Fila, Puma, Lotto, Nike, Adidas, and ASICS, workers reported: *'Pretty girls in the factory are always harassed by the male managers. They come on to the girls, call them into their offices, whisper into their ears, touch them at the waist, arms, neck, buttocks, and breasts, bribe the girls with money and threats of losing their jobs to have sex with them.'* Women workers in particular experience a high level of harassment where it is seen as culturally acceptable for male supervisors and managers to treat women in an abusive way.

Trade unions undermined

The ability to join and form a trade union remains a great challenge in the sportswear production sector. In all four of the researched sportswear factories in Turkey producing collectively for Lotto, Fila, Puma, and Kappa, no unions were allowed. In one of the factories producing for Puma in Bulgaria,[12] it was reported that management had a hostile attitude towards any form of worker representation in the enterprise.

The obstacles to forming and joining a trade union are sometimes exacerbated by governments when they undermine workers' rights as a means of attracting foreign investment. Sometimes the employers harass and discriminate against those who join in union activities. Added to this, long working hours leave little time for workers to engage in trade-union organising; and workers refrain from participating because they are afraid that union membership will threaten their jobs.

In many of the factories that we researched, workers reported that management made it clear that union organising was not acceptable. Workers interviewed in these factories felt convinced that joining a union would lead to being fired. Rana, a 22-year-old garment worker in Turkish Factory W, producing for Lotto and Puma, told researchers: *'Last year while the workers of the next factory were striking in front of their factory, our supervisor said to us "You will see – all of them will lose their jobs. You never make this mistake. Otherwise you also face the same consequence.",* A young female worker from a Cambodian sportswear factory[13] producing for Fila and Puma reported that there was no union at her factory, and that workers did not dare to protest over anything for fear of losing their jobs. She also said that the employers discriminated against unionists: if a factory manager finds out that a job applicant has been involved in union activities, the applicant will not be employed. One Indonesian worker described what happened after a strike at a factory[14] producing for Umbro and Reebok:

'The strike organisers were initially suspended. They were not allowed to come to work and received only 75 per cent of their standard wages. They were consequently all fired. We felt very scared and powerless when this happened. It was like a slap; it was as if the management were saying to us: "See, this is the consequence of your strike". The constant intimidation by the management gives us no chance to feel empowered.'

Many of the workers interviewed expressed their belief that trade-union representation would give them the bargaining power necessary to change the unhealthy and undignified working conditions in their factories. Yet this means of achieving justice is continually threatened by employers and also by governments. Although freedom of association and collective bargaining is protected as a constitutional right in many countries, governments often allow employers to flout it in order to offer cheaper labour to global buyers. Whether through changes to the law – for example, in a number of countries, the rights to unionise and strike are prohibited by law in export-processing zones – *or de facto* through non-enforcement, thousands of workers across the globe are unfairly denied the opportunity to defend their rights.

There is clear evidence of violations of trade union rights in this sector in all the countries mentioned in this report. The ICFTU produces an annual worldwide survey of trade union rights. Further details are given in the appendix.

BOX 3: Fundamental principles and rights at work

In 1998, the International Labour Organization produced the Declaration on Fundamental Principles and Rights at Work. In the declaration, ILO member states agreed that they should all respect, promote, and realise these core labour standards as embodied in key ILO conventions:

Freedom of association and the effective recognition of the right to collective bargaining (Convention No. 87 & No. 98)

The elimination of all forms of forced and compulsory labour (Convention No. 29 & No. 105)

The effective abolition of child labour (Convention No. 138 & No. 182)

The elimination of discrimination in respect of employment and occupation (Convention No. 100 & No. 111)

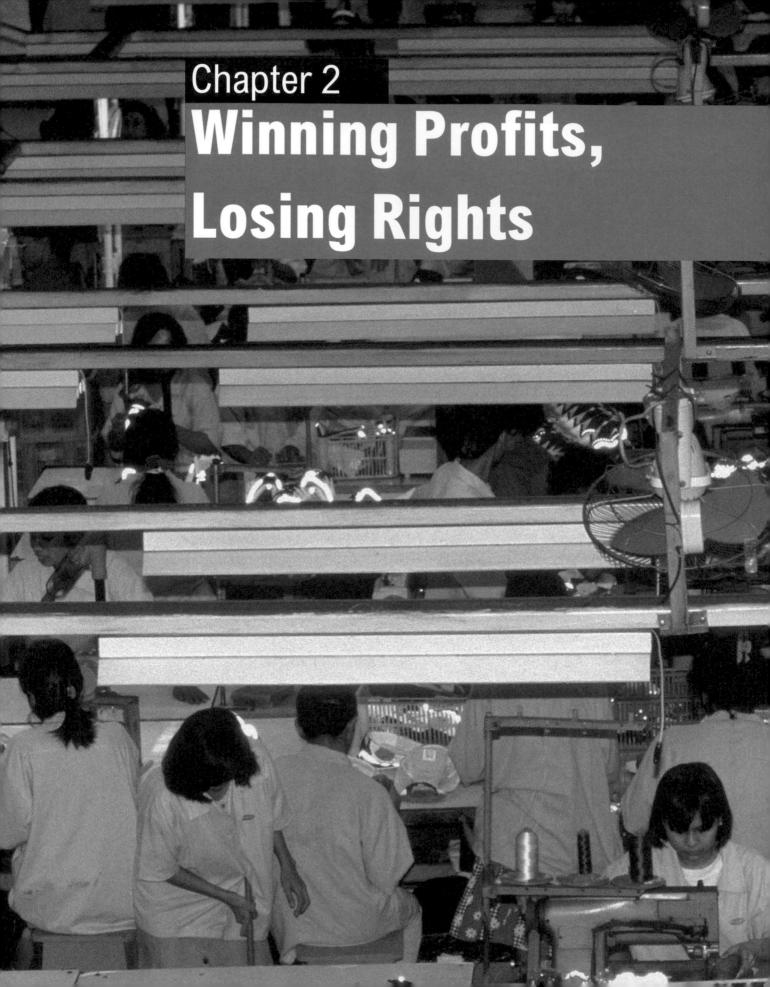

Chapter 2
Winning Profits, Losing Rights

Producing trainers for the export market in Indonesia

2: Winning Profits, Losing Rights

Many sportswear companies recognise that there are bad labour practices in their supply-chain. Their response to criticism has been to adopt codes of conduct covering labour practices, which have led to limited improvements.
What is not acknowledged openly is the role that the company itself plays in causing the problem. Our research shows that driving the harsh, abusive, and exploitative working conditions in the sportswear industry is a business model designed to bring products to the marketplace speedily and cheaply.

To deliver this model, suppliers must be able to meet faster delivery times, keep labour costs low, and be flexible to respond to the fluctuating size and frequency of orders being placed by global brands. Factory managers respond by pushing their workers to work faster and for longer periods of time; by keeping their wages down in order to maximise their own profits and to meet prices offered by the brands; and by preventing them – through intimidation and other means – from challenging any abusive or unfair treatment, resulting in the kinds of experience described in the previous chapter. Governments, through their failure to enact or enforce workers' rights, make it easier for unscrupulous employers to adjust to market pressures by cutting corners – and costs – through the erosion of workers' rights.

Violations of trade-union rights have helped create the conditions for the spread of the new business model. The odds are stacked against trade unions, either through union-busting policies adopted by employers – often with the tacit support of governments – or through difficulties in recruiting members, if workers are too scared to organise for fear of losing their jobs or being harassed or physically attacked, or they are too exhausted by long working hours. Under these circumstances, employers have gained a *carte blanche* to treat workers badly with impunity.

This section sheds light on this model and explains how it operates in the supply-chains of big global sportswear brands, and why it is translating into abusive and exploitative terms and conditions of employment for the many workers at the end of the production line.

The global sportswear industry

The shift from the marketing of sportswear as specialist performance items to promoting it as mainstream fashion items for the general public has greatly benefited the sportswear industry, drawing in young purchasers and expanding its consumer base. In 2002, the athletic apparel and footwear market was worth more than US$ 58 billion. The top three companies – Nike, Reebok, and Adidas – reaped pre-tax profits amounting to US$ 1123 million, US$ 195.5 million, and US$ 408.9 million respectively.

BOX 4: Profit boom: pre-tax profits of seven sportswear companies

Nike	US$ 1,123 million (2003)
Adidas	US$ 408.9 million (2002)
Reebok	US$ 195.5 million (2002)
Puma	US$ 320 million (2003)
ASICS	US$ 51.7 million (2003)
BasicNet/Kappa	US$ 7.5 million (2002)
Lotto	US$ 6.4 million (2002)

It is, however, a highly competitive market. The race is intense among the companies to deliver products at competitive prices, which meet demands of fashion and quality and at the same time maximise returns to shareholders. To compete, sportswear companies have invested in strong branding and marketing to capture and retain customers. Advertising and promotional spending alone in 2002[15] cost Nike US$ 1,028 million. The expenditure of others has been more modest, but figures still run into the millions, with Adidas spending US$ 775 million, Puma US$ 107 million, Mizuno US$ 81.6 million and Fila US$ 72 million. A great proportion of these budgets is spent on sponsorship and endorsement deals of sportsmen and women. In the run-up to the Athens Olympic Games, the top brands will be launching state-of-the-art products and running huge advertising campaigns to boost their exposure. This marketing campaign will include selling products which carry the Olympics emblem, outfitting those athletes or teams whom they sponsor, and supplying Olympics officials with services and products.

BOX 5: The cost of celebrity sponsorship deals

David Beckham, football (Adidas)
US$ 161 million over his lifetime

Grant Hill, basketball (Fila)
US$ 7 million (1997 – 2004)

Venus Williams, tennis (Reebok)
US$ 38 million over five years

Marion Jones, running (Nike)
US$ 800,000 per year

Mark Phelps, swimming (Speedo)
US$ 300,000 a year

BOX 6: Making money from the Olympics

Since the Los Angeles Summer Olympics of 1980, corporate sponsorship has become an integral part of the Olympic Games. Originally intended as an philanthropic gesture when government funding for the event declined, sponsoring the Olympics now brings in big money. According to the official website of the 2004 Olympics, by December 2003 sponsorship revenues had reached US$ 648 million, with cash coming from multinationals like Coca-cola, Swatch, and McDonald's, in addition to an array of Greek companies. Sponsorship is also provided in kind. For example, Adidas is the official sponsor of Sport Clothing for Uniforms at the Athens 2004, while Mizuno supplies the International Olympics Committee and the Athens Organising Committee with their official clothing for all Olympic events. Although the actual gains of co-branding with the Olympics are intangible, companies have clearly calculated their returns on the millions of dollars that they spend on it.

Marketing is the other big money-maker of the Olympic Games. The movement, through the International Olympics Committee (IOC), the National Olympics Committees (NOCs), and the Organising Committees (OCOGs), licenses companies to produce and market Olympics souvenirs such as caps, sweatshirts, and T-shirts. Upon payment of a royalty fee, companies gain the right to use the Olympics emblem on their merchandise. From the games in Athens 2004, royalty revenues are expected to generate around US$ 66 million. For companies, the publicity and sales that result from retailing Olympics merchandise are a lucrative business. Roots, the Canadian clothing company that sponsors the US, Canadian, and British Olympic teams, sells replicas of the teams' kits in High Street shops. The company is already planning to open some 100 stores in China by 2006. Sportswear companies also gain financially from sponsoring national Olympic teams. At the 2002 Salt Lake City Winter Olympics, Roots supplied the official team uniforms for the Canadian, US, and British teams. In the two-week period of the Games, Roots' sales exceeded US$ 25 million.

Figure 1: Bargaining power within the supply-chain

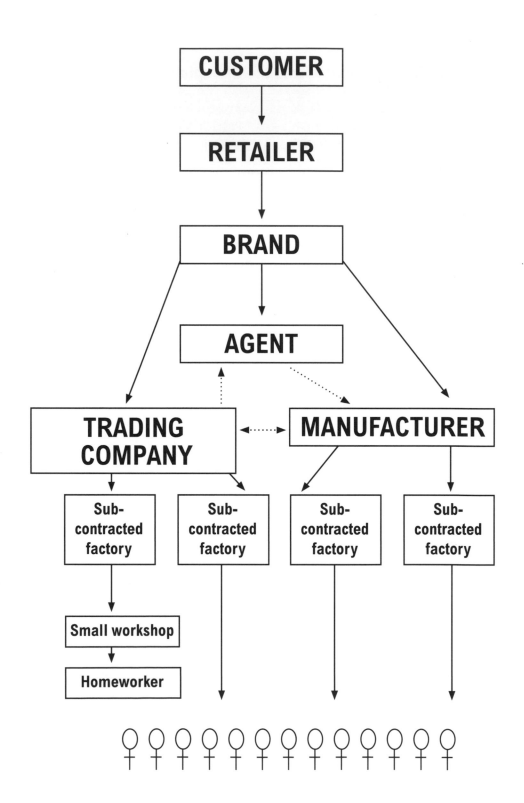

Retailers – like Footlocker, Decathlon, and Wal-Mart – use their huge bargaining power over the brands to reduce the cost-price of products. The retailers' negotiating strength derives from providing the brands with access to consumers. Dominating the supply-chain, they rake in huge profits; for example, **Foot Locker's sales in 2002 were US$ 4.5 billion. Its operating profit was US$ 269 million.**

Sports-brands such as Puma and Fila retain the high-profit inputs such as design, marketing, and retailing, while outsourcing the low-profit steps such as production, assembly, finishing, and packaging to manufacturers in low-cost locations. This segmenting of the production cycle has proved to be a successful profit-making model, with large global brands raking in profits amounting to hundreds of millions of dollars; **for example, Puma's sales in 2002 were US$ 1.154 billion, and its operating profit was US$ 159 million.** These brands wield immense negotiating strength over their suppliers, because they provide access to the global marketplace.

Trading companies are contracted by the brands to deliver a total production package comprising sourcing of raw materials, production planning and management, packaging, export administration, and freighting. Where brands have chosen to use them, they deal directly with the factory owners and are responsible for making sure that the product is delivered on time, at the right price, and at the right quality. Many of these trading companies began as manufacturers but, with the growing use of outsourcing, they have changed roles to capitalise on a new market. The Hong Kong-owned Li & Fung, for example, contracts other independent manufacturers. Seeking to take their own – large - share of the profit, these mid-chain players bargain hard with the manufacturers on price. **In 2002, Li & Fung's turnover was US$ 4.8 billion and its operating profit was US$ 146 million.**

Manufacturers are contracted either directly by the brands or through an **agent** or trading company. Some, like the large Taiwanese-owned Pou Chen Group, are multinational companies in themselves. The company still has its own production facilities (based in this case in China, Indonesia, and Vietnam). **Pou Chen's turnover was US$ 1,939 million, and operating profit was US$ 229 million.** Others are much smaller and their bargaining power is relatively weak in comparison, given that there are huge numbers of them in many low-cost countries, seeking to supply the big global brands. **In 2002, a large Chinese manufacturer had sales of US$ 50.7 million and an operating profit of US$ 8.9 million.** They are the direct employers of the workers who sew and assemble the branded apparel and sports-shoes. Often, these manufacturers will sub-contract other smaller factories to help them to fulfil production orders. These **sub-contracted factories** have even less ability to negotiate on price and time; usually working conditions are worse on these sites, as the risks are passed on to the workers.

Workers are at the bottom of the supply-chain. They have the weakest bargaining power, especially when they are prevented from organising and using their collective bargaining rights. They receive a very small cut of the profits along the supply-chain. The typical annual wage of a Cambodian garment worker in 2003 was approximately US$ 1,500: 0.0009 per cent of Puma's annual profits in 2002.

Making money in a competitive market

But customers want a bargain. In the last five years, the prices of athletic footwear and apparel have gradually fallen to meet both consumer demand and pressure from sportswear retailers such as Foot-Locker, Intersport, Decathlon, and others. Whereas in 1997 the average price for a pair of trainers in the USA was US$ 41, in 2002 it was down to US$ 36.[16] To maintain and increase profitability in a difficult business environment, companies have sought to rigorously strip out costs from their supply-chains. Outsourcing production to others, while retaining higher-value inputs like design and marketing, continues to be a favoured option. Advanced communication technologies and cheaper transport costs have also allowed these companies to scour the world looking for suppliers who are prepared to supply them at the lowest price.

Long and complex production-chains are typical in the industry, though more so in the production of apparel than shoes.[17] Sportswear companies place a great many orders with an increasingly concentrated number of agents and supply-chain managers, who in turn farm them out to a wide network of manufacturers and subcontractors.[18] The bargaining power of the different players varies vastly, as shown in Figure 1. Some of the players within the supply-chain are big multinational companies in themselves. For example, Taiwanese footwear manufacturer, Pou Chen, has an estimated 16 per cent share of the global footwear market, receiving orders from 30 different global sportswear brands including Nike, Reebok, Adidas, ASICS, and Puma. In 2002, the company had some 205,000 workers in its employment, working in an array of production sites located in a number of East-Asian countries.[19]

The typical business model used by global sports-brands involves strategies designed to achieve the following objectives:

▶ deliver products efficiently and speedily to retail outlets;

▶ keep down production costs – including labour costs – in order to maximise profit;

▶ minimise inventory costs by shifting packing, warehousing, and freighting functions to the supplier;

▶ and shift the risks arising from poor forecasting of consumer demand to the supplier.

The model thrives upon the immense power and negotiating strength that a small number of big global brands – and, to an extent, a few powerful mid-supply-chain players – are able to exert over their wide range of potential suppliers, especially those at the low end of the supply chain. An important new trend to consider is that higher up in the supply chain many of the primarily East-Asian companies have become huge transnationals themselves owning factories or subcontracting orders globally so they share a responsability with the global brands when it comes to changing sourcing practices. Desperate to gain a foothold in the global marketplace, garment and footwear manufacturers, many based in the developing world, strive to offer the cheapest deals, in the shortest production times, in the most flexible manner, to the big brands.

How buyers buy

The sportswear business model also thrives on the huge pressure felt by buying and merchandising staff in the big companies to deliver to very demanding deadlines and tight budgets. Often young and seeking to prove themselves within the business as a means of climbing the corporate ladder, sportswear buyers work very competitively to meet their performance targets: getting the best price, in the best time, and at the best quality. In a few companies, buyers are given some training to introduce them to the companies' ethical commitments, but there is usually little attempt to integrate these commitments into the buyers' role. So much so that in an independent piece of research carried out recently, researchers found that buyers sometimes referred to their colleagues in the Ethical or Corporate Social Responsibility Team as the 'Sales Prevention Team'.[20]

Our research shows that buyers are generally adopting the following purchasing practices to keep delivery lead-times short and prices low, and to maintain flexibility in meeting supply and demand.[21]

Placing smaller orders more frequently
The traditional system of ordering in bulk to meet consumer demands in the basic four seasons has dramatically altered. For one thing, the number of fashion seasons has increased. For another, bar-coding systems track consumer purchases, allowing retailers to order stock automatically as it runs out in stores. So instead of ordering in bulk from suppliers and then keeping supplies in stock, either in the shop or in the warehouse, at huge cost, the purchaser expects the supplier to deliver smaller amounts to replenish the shop-shelves as and when they become empty. This system also protects the companies from the problem of surplus stock if products

Sewing sportswear for export in Thailand

prove to be unsuccessful. Recently, the general manager for Nike in Bangkok was quoted[22] as saying: *'Thai factories receive orders for Nike products on a monthly basis, but this is expected to change to a weekly order system as customers become more demanding.'* For the suppliers, it means having to deliver smaller orders in less time and according to very tight export deadlines. If they fail to do so, they incur fines and other penalties such as heavier freighting charges. At Indonesian factory D, producing for ASICS, Fila, Lotto, Puma, and Nike, workers reported being forced to work for as long as 24 consecutive hours during export periods. They complained to management that such overtime is against the law, but were told that if the goods did not reach the loading dock at a fixed time, the factory would be fined several million rupiah – and, as this would be the workers' fault, they would have to bear the cost.

Pushing for shorter delivery lead-times
All the major sports-brands have prioritised shortening the time taken to deliver a product from the factory to the shop-shelf. As the General Manager for Global Sourcing at Puma says: *'Lead-times are today important. Here we try to shorten lead-times in order to become competitive. Especially in that area where fashion brands are working with very short lead-times, we have to compete with them.*[23] At Adidas, the 2002 annual report states that the company aims to reduce lead-time for apparel from 120 days to 90 days. Unless production planning at the supplier level is simultaneously adjusted to meet this target, the risk is that an even greater pressure is placed upon employees to work long overtime hours to meet export deadlines.

Lowering unit costs
Across the board, researchers for this report found that the unit cost per item of footwear or clothing in the sportswear sector has fallen year on year. In Honduras, two factories producing T-shirts for export for famous sports-brands reported that the price paid per dozen by the sourcing company had fallen from US$ 3.70 in 2000 to US$ 2.85 in 2003: a fall of 23 per cent in three years. In Indonesian factory D, producing for Nike, Fila, ASICS, Lotto, and Puma, one worker said: *'The manager in our division often uses this [the fall in unit prices] as a reason why our standard monthly wages can't be increased.'* The owner of factory M in China, producing for Umbro, confirmed that the unit prices for Umbro shoes were falling. In his factory, workers complained that their wages had dramatically fallen, compared with three years ago. Back then the factory at least paid them the minimum wage during the low season, but even this protection has now been removed. In September 2003, workers in the sole department were paid between RMB 200 and RMB 400 (US$ 24-48) – below the legal minimum set by the province.

While prices fall, conversely production costs for the factories are rising. The owner of a Sri Lankan factory supplying to Nike[24] estimated that while production costs had increased by approximately 20 per cent in the last five years, unit prices paid by Nike had dropped by 35 per cent in the previous 18 months. He says: *'I feel that prices are reaching rock-bottom now in Sri Lanka, and I am not sure how we will survive.'*

Threatening to relocate
The threat of buyers moving to other locations where operating costs are lower has also exerted a downward pressure on price. The owner of a large Cambodian sportswear factory[25] told researchers: *'They always compare the price in Cambodia with those other countries [Viet Nam, China, and Bangladesh].'* He said that the buyers regularly note that sourcing goods in Cambodia is more expensive, and they put pressure on factories to adjust their prices accordingly. He claims that on average the unit cost of one particular item produced in his factory had fallen from $US 12 in 2000 to US$ 7 in 2003, in order to meet competition from cheaper sources.

In many cases, relocation to cheaper production sites does actually happen. This is particularly true within the apparel sector. Unlike the shoe sector, where brands tend to build longer relationships with those factories that have developed technical expertise and capacity, it is easy for buyers to switch apparel suppliers, simply on the basis of cost. One supplier to Nike told researchers that the increasing demands for lower prices became so unrealistic that he finally terminated the relationship. He claims that Nike relocated production for that product to Viet Nam for a difference in cost which amounted to a mere US$ 0.40 per piece.[26]

Flex and squeeze: the supplier's response

Under these pressures, suppliers are generally not respecting labour standards in their workplace. They are working their workers harder, paying them less, shifting liabilities on to them, and preventing them from demanding better wages and conditions. Desperate to enter the supply-chains of global brands, factory managers agree to tight deadlines, fluctuating orders, and low unit costs, knowing that they can make their workers deliver despite the adverse personal effects on them. Hence the kinds of abuse and exploitation documented in Chapter 1. The sourcing companies take advantage of this desperation, with little regard for its impact on those who actually produce the sportswear that carries their brand. Our research indicates that the factory managers are using the following workforce-management tactics.

Hiring women, migrants, and temporary workers

A common trend within the industry is to hire workers who seem less likely to challenge management in the face of unfair and difficult working conditions. More and more, factories are using temporary workers (see Chapter 1). Without regular contracts or any guarantee of job security, temporary workers are more willing to comply with employers' demands. As they are paid on piece-rate and often at low rates per piece, they are willing to work as long as it takes to earn a decent wage. Finally, without a sense of permanence in the workplace and a fear of being fired, they are reluctant to join trade-union activities. For management, temporary – and therefore disposable – workers are the easiest solution to the need to expand and contract the workforce to accommodate fluctuating orders. Migrant workers are even more vulnerable. Far from home, often not speaking the local language or dialect, and sometimes undocumented, they are unlikely to challenge management, for fear of losing their jobs or being reported to the authorities.

In the nine Indonesian sportswear factories where workers were interviewed for this report, the average ratio was seven women to each man. When asked the reason for the predominance of women workers, workers cited three reasons: traditional patriarchal values, economic discrimination, and gender-based skills. A 21-year-old woman worker from Indonesian sportswear factory H said: *'We women follow orders more than men do, because we are already used to following orders from our fathers, brothers and husbands. So the manager just becomes another man to follow orders from.'* The industry also accepts without question that women can be paid less than men, because their incomes are often seen as supplementary to those of the male bread-winners. In actual fact, women workers in the sportswear industry are often the sole income-providers in their households. A garment worker in Indonesian sportswear factory E told researchers: *'Women in our culture are supposed to be housewives, taken care of by their husbands, which makes the economic role in the family, the men's role.'* A worker from Indonesian sportswear factory H says that the reason why factories pay women less is that *'The managers assume that health-care costs of women will be automatically taken care of when she gets married.'* Many employers also justify their dismissals of women workers on the basis that their responsibilities at home – as mothers, wives, daughters, care-givers and home-makers – make them inefficient in the workplace, given the erratic working hours.

Women workers do try to improve their situation, often at great personal risk, but they encounter many obstacles when they try to join or form trade unions. At two Indonesian factories[27] producing predominantly for Nike, women workers said that the traditional attitudes towards women's roles made it difficult for them to become active union members. Married women, for example, are expected to fulfil the main childcare and household responsibilities, despite long working hours – a fact which leaves them little time for trade-union activities.

Short lead times, long working hours

As evidenced in Chapter 1, long working hours and compulsory overtime are used as a matter of course to meet shortened lead-times. Workers from factories supplying sports-brands reported working days ranging from 13 to 24 hours, with work on both Saturdays and Sundays during export deadline periods. In all cases, overtime is compulsory.

Payment by piece, excessive targets

Workers – especially those on short-term, temporary contracts – are usually paid on piece-rate in the sportswear industry: they earn according to the number of pieces that they produce, rather than a standard weekly or monthly wage. In order to be paid, workers have to meet a target amount set by the managers. If workers fail to meet the target, they are sometimes not paid at all and are commonly expected to complete the target during unpaid overtime hours. This method of payment has the following advantages for factory managers:

▶ it allows them to reduce labour costs when orders and unit prices are low;

▶ they can make workers work harder, because the more they make, the more they earn – a tactic that is especially useful in meeting short lead-times;

▶ they can avoid overtime payments by setting excessive targets.

A 21-year-old worker in Indonesian sportswear factory I, supplying Umbro, told researchers: '*If you don't reach production targets, you are forced to do unpaid overtime ... You have to reach a certain target to make the minimum wage. If you don't, there are two sanctions: work unpaid overtime or get graded with a "zero" on your production report. If you get graded "zero" too many times, you get a warning letter. Too many warning letters, and you are demoted. If the worker is demoted, the management will move her around the factory until she is so embarrassed that she resigns.*'

'Supervisors use stopwatches to count the minutes it takes us to complete tasks ...Many workers are getting sick because they have to stop themselves from going to the toilets because the targets are so high that they would not meet them if they took this break.'

(Jamal, a worker in Indonesian factory E, producing for Nike)

Often, factory managers set excessive targets. Workers in a Bulgarian factory[28] producing for Puma said that the targets in their factory were often unachievable within a normal working day. As they were paid by the piece, this then affected the wage they received. Workers in this factory said that this wage was not enough to pay for their individual subsistence as well as meeting their household budgets. Some factory managers also alter the targets according to the fluctuating orders, thus controlling their labour costs during peak and low seasons. Elsa, a garment worker in Indonesian factory D supplying Lotto, Puma, Fila, ASICS, Nike, and Adidas products, told researchers: *'In the garment division, the usual target is a thousand pieces per lane, per day. But during export days, the target doubles to two thousand pieces. This doubling is very stressful for us, and we often cannot reach it. When we don't reach it, we get yelled at by the management and sometimes we get warning letters.'* In Chinese factory N, producing for Mizuno and Kappa, managers reduced the amount paid for each piece when they wanted workers to meet higher targets.

BOX 7: Mara's story

Mara is a 25-year-old Cambodian garment worker, sewing products for Adidas. She moved away from her village in a rural province to look for garment work in Phnom Penh in order to support her widowed mother and six siblings, following the death of her father. She told researchers about the pressure at the factory:

'Our supervisor asks us to work faster, to sew accurately, and to meet the targets set. My target is 120 trousers per hour. For this, I earn between US$ 1.25 and $1.50. In the normal working day I have to sew 960 pairs. If I do not meet this, my monthly incentive bonus of US$ 5 is cut. I even hold off from going to the bathroom to meet my target.

When we want to go to the bathroom during working hours, the supervisor must stamp our production cards.

'Overtime starts at 4 pm and runs till 6 pm. Sometimes we don't stop till 8 pm. If I work that late, I am frightened of the dark. Many motodup (motorbike taxis) ask to take me home. I do not want to go with them, so I run back to my room.

'If I work all the overtime shifts, I get around US$ 60-65 per month. If not, I get around US$ 55. Of this, I spend US$ 5 on rent for my room and send between US$ 10 and $20 to my family. The rest goes on food and medicine. I cannot save anything from my salary.'

Low orders, low wages

When orders are low, however, the opposite tactic is taken by management as a means of cutting costs: workers are forced to take unpaid leave. *'Right now the orders are so low that last week we had Tuesday off, and this week we had Wednesday off. We do not receive wages for the days off. But when orders are high, we often have to work on Sundays too,'* says Aminah from a factory[29] producing for Umbro and Puma.

Even for those workers who are not forced to take leave, wages often fall to a minimum, or they receive nothing at all during the low season. In a number of Chinese factories where sports-brand products are made, workers have to cut back on basic needs or borrow money. A worker in the sole department of Factory L, manufacturing Umbro products, said: *'We did not have many orders in September. Most of us received only RMB 400–500 (US$ 48–60) [that month]. Some received only RMB 100 (US$ 12). The lowest wage paid in our department was RMB 45 (US$ 5)! After deducting food and lodging, our wage was pathetic.'* At another Chinese factory[30] producing for Umbro and Diadora, workers were receiving only between RMB 200 and 300 (US$ 24–36) per month, even though the legal minimum wage in that city was RMB 320 (US$ 38) per month.

You fine us, we fine them

As factory managers face all manner of penalties from the buyers – fines for late delivery, contributions when the product does not do well in the shops, and penalties if the product is sub-standard – so they try to shift some of their liabilities on to the workers. In China, workers at one factory[31] went on a two-day strike when management imposed huge fines on them for mistakes made on the soles of Umbro shoes. The deductions from their wages were made during a low-order period, when wages were already very low. At another factory[32] also producing for Umbro in China, management systematically demand a deduction from wages amounting to between RMB 20 and 30 (US$ 2.40–3.60) for a 'material replenishment fee', if extra materials have been brought in to fix faulty products. In September 2003, each worker incurred a fee of RMB 100 (US$ 12), which caused great discontent, leading to a strike. Although in both cases the management relented and paid back the deduction, this practice of imposing fines for flawed products has not ended. At a third factory[33] producing also for Umbro as well as for Fila, stitchers report being fined a minimum of RMB 50 (US$ 6) for every faulty product. These same workers had a regular working day of 12 hours. Some of them worked on a night shift from 7.30 pm to 7.30 am.

Prevent organising

As evidenced in Chapter 1, workers are actively discouraged from forming and joining trade unions in many sportswear factories. Suppliers do not want to be challenged about their frequent breaches of laws concerning overtime work and payments, wage regulations, and health and safety standards in their workplaces. Apart from the increased and regular scrutiny of labour practices that the presence of trade unions would bring, losing their freedom to abuse workers reduces the factory manager's capacity to meet the demands of the buyers and win a share of the profit.

Whose responsibility?

Suppliers – as employers – have a direct legal and moral responsibility to ensure that their workers are treated decently, employed under fair terms, and work in healthy and safe circumstances. Many are failing to meet their obligations. Too often, the factories are poorly managed. Faced with increasing demands for speed, flexibility, and lower costs, many owners pursue short-term solutions to meet the orders of their buyers and secure their share of the profits by callously shifting the risks and costs down to the workers. The extreme working hours and excessive targets imposed on workers in the rush to meet export deadlines are partly a symptom of deficient production planning. A worker at a factory[34] producing for Fila, Puma, Lotto, and ASICS, where targets were doubled from 1000 to 2000 pieces to meet export deadlines, said: *'This last-minute panic is the fault of the management. They accept production orders that are too large, and they don't employ enough workers in the factory.'*

However, if manufacturers are to invest in improving their production planning and worker management, the overwhelming pressure currently placed upon them by the sportswear companies must be diffused. Continual downward squeezes on price and increased demands for speed and flexibility leave factory managers little room to improve working conditions in their factories.

This responsibility also attaches to the large multinational manufacturers – like Pou Chen – and trading companies – like Li & Fung – who sit mid-chain and often place the direct pressure in terms of price and delivery upon the factory managers.

Many of the sportswear companies mentioned in this report have issued codes of conduct covering labour practices, obliging their suppliers to ensure respect for their workers' rights. These codes, however, assume that it is mainly the factory managers' responsibility to take steps towards this end. Even if the factories do meet these standards, there is no guarantee that they will continue to receive business. As one factory owner in Cambodia told researchers: *'High labour standards in Cambodia do not tie a buyer to a factory. Only a good price can do that.'* Further, as these sportswear companies scour the world for new low-cost, 'one-stop shop' manufacturing locations to maximise profits for the benefits of their shareholders, so they forgo their commitment to a long-term business relationship with their suppliers, thus condemning workers to the added stress of job insecurity.

Some of the more enlightened companies are beginning to see that unless they acknowledge their part in causing unhealthy, unsafe, and unfair working conditions through aggressive purchasing practices, the chances of addressing the problems to any significant extent are low. For example, the Global Director for Social and Environmental Affairs at Adidas acknowledges: *'If a factory manager says "we cannot comply [with social standards] because your order arrived yesterday to deliver this morning", we have to review our internal processes'.*[35] Other companies, unfortunately, are indifferent to concerns that their purchasing practices are undermining their ethical commitments.

Ultimately, governments too have a responsibility to ensure that workers are accorded those rights enshrined in the Conventions of the International Labour Organization (ILO). Evidence in this report reveals a failure to provide adequate labour protection for thousands of workers who support national economies through making sports shoes, apparel, and other accessories for export. Governments – in pursuing export-led growth – have adjusted their labour policies to meet the requirements of global sourcing companies. With encouragement from international financial institutions like the International Monetary Fund (IMF) and the World Bank, policies to create 'labour market flexibility' have been put in place, leading to the erosion of workers' rights.[36] Human rights such as the right to freedom of association and the right to collective bargaining have been undermined, in order to prevent workers from banding together to demand better wages and terms of employment. Governments turn a blind eye when employers avoid their obligations through the use of temporary and casual workers which, among other things, makes it easy to dismiss them without having to make severance payments. Legal working hours have been extended in certain sectors like garment and footwear manufacturing. Even where good labour laws exist on paper, enforcement is weak.

Box 8: Respect the rules

Rules to protect the rights of workers are some of the oldest in the world. Today, 195 ILO conventions have been adopted, providing an array of protection to workers worldwide, ranging from fundamental basic human rights such as freedom of association, the right to organise, collective bargaining, abolition of forced labour, equality of opportunity and treatment, and the outlawing of child labour to more detailed provisions such as maternity protection and health and safety regulations. Many of these international standards have been translated into national legislation. Inherent in these laws is the obligation upon governments to adopt mechanisms to ensure that workers are protected, to establish trade unions to protect and defend their interests, and to provide means of challenging breaches and gaining reparation for wrong-doing. Sadly, however, the gap between the letter and the practice of the law is far too wide in many countries. The ICFTU's annual survey of violations of trade-union rights 2003 shows how fundamental rights enshrined in the ILO Conventions are flouted in countries around the world, depriving millions of workers of their rights to trade-union representation, and thus their ability to demand decent working conditions. Across all the countries researched for this report, employers within the sportswear-manufacturing industry are getting away with:

► preventing union members from exercising their rights to strike, to join unions, or to bargain collectively, as stipulated by constitution or labour laws;

► demanding working hours far in excess of the maximum set by legislation;

► not paying workers the legal minimum wage nor overtime wages according to the calculations set by law;

► imposing illegal penalties and fines upon workers;

► not issuing proper employment contracts;

► discriminating against certain groups of workers; and

► seriously breaching health and safety regulations.

The trade-union movement – globally and locally – has persistently challenged the failures of governments. In recent years, it has had some successes in strengthening enforcement, amending laws that violate workers' rights, and changing policies that contravene labour protection. For example, in Bangladesh, as a result of persistent campaigning by international and national trade-union bodies, the government has given an undertaking to extend the National Labour Code to all its export-processing zones by the middle of 2004. But much more needs to change, if workers are to be adequately protected.

Fair play for workers

It is in the interests of the sporting world to put pressure on the sportswear industry to respect labour standards. So intrinsically linked is the practice of sport with the sports-brands that any taint on the industry's reputation also stains the reputation of the sports institutions. Yet the sporting world – apart from a few exceptions – has done very little to call for change on the part of the sportswear companies, despite years of campaigning.

BOX 9: Glimmers of hope

Respect for workers' rights at the Sydney Olympics

The organising committee for the Olympic and Paralympic Games in Sydney 2000 adopted a Code of Labour Practice for the production of licensed Olympic goods. The Code – negotiated with the Australian Council of Trade Unions (ACTU) and the Labour Council of New South Wales in 1998 – required the payment of fair wages, limitations on working hours, and respect for the rights of freedom of association and collective bargaining. The compliance measures in the initial agreement were weak; the agreement relied on the organising committees themselves to enforce the code, rather than commissioning bodies with expertise in workers' rights. After much campaigning by Australian unions, in 1999 the organising committees signed an agreement with the Textile Clothing and Footwear Union of Australia, giving the union the right of access to information about workplaces and the right to send representatives to speak to workers. Unfortunately by this time most of the garments for the Sydney Olympics had already been made. The code has, however, been linked to improvements for workers in at least one country. Following lobbying by Australian and Fijian unions, union officials were allowed to visit two factories in Fiji which were producing shirts for the Sydney Olympics. As a result, those two factories became unionised, and the workers negotiated significant pay rises. Similarly, other unions, including construction, transport, and public-sector unions, were able to strike agreements which provided respect for workers' rights and facilitated a genuine partnership with working Australians that was vital for the success of the games.

FIFA commitments on labour standards in the production of soccer balls

In mid-1996, the international trade-union movement uncovered evidence, supported by video footage, that child labour was being used to manufacture soccer balls bearing what appeared to be the logo of FIFA, the football world's governing body. The balls were being made in the town of Sialkot, Pakistan, the source of some three-quarters of the world's soccer balls at that time. The discovery was made just before the start of the 1996 European Championships and received extensive worldwide media coverage. The ICFTU, working with the Global Union organisations for the textiles sector (ITGLWF) and retail sector (UNI), approached the European and world governing bodies for soccer (UEFA and FIFA), seeking to reach agreement on a set of criteria to ensure respect for fundamental workers' rights in their licensing agreements.

On 3 September 1996, FIFA agreed to a 'Code of Labour Practice' for FIFA-licensed products, as requested by the trade unions. Labour-standards criteria – based on the ILO Declaration on Fundamental Principles and Rights at Work – have now been included in the licensing agreements. The Clean Clothes Campaign has, however, repeatedly targeted FIFA for not implementing this code, presenting it with evidence of non-compliance.

A code for the sporting-goods industry

The World Federation of Sporting Goods Industry (WSFGI) is an independent association formed by the industry suppliers, national organisations, and businesses related to the sporting-goods industry. Its membership includes global sports-brands, retailers, and manufacturers of sportswear and sporting goods. In 2000, it introduced a revised Code of Conduct based on the international labour standards outlined in the key ILO Conventions. The preamble to the Code states: *'WFSGI members recognize the important role they play in the global economy and their influence on the social and economic conditions under which sporting goods are manufactured and produced. That influence is exercised both through their actions as employers and far more profoundly through their decisions as customers of companies that serve as suppliers of goods and services.'* The Code commits members to take steps to ensure compliance with the Code within their own operations, as well as the operations of those that supply them. Although the Code is comprehensive on paper, the WFSGI has done little to ensure that members implement it.

The Olympics movement is a particularly stark example of this indifference. In spite of its rhetorical commitments to fair play, international solidarity, and valuing the worth of human beings, it has not taken any practical action at the global level to challenge the sportswear brands on the exploitative and abuse working conditions in their supply-chains.

As the leading governing body in world sport, the International Olympics Committee (IOC) has a moral and legal obligation to make these calls. Their obligation includes making sure that companies that use the Olympics logo respect fundamental workers' rights. To date, however, the IOC has done little apart from 'encourage' the efforts of the World Federation for Sporting Goods Industry (WFSGI) in this area. This lack of commitment seems irresponsible, particularly given that the officials' uniforms, parade uniforms of the various national Olympics teams, athletes' kits, and souvenir sportswear, all bearing the Olympics emblem, may well be produced under the kinds of exploitative working conditions described in this report. Currently, those sportswear companies that act as official suppliers of uniforms or kit to the IOC (for example, Mizuno, the supplier of official clothing to IOC officials) or to the organising committee of the host nation (for example, Adidas, as the official sponsor of Sport Clothing for Uniforms at the Athens 2004), or the national Olympics teams through their national Olympics committees are under no obligation to ensure that these products are not made by exploited workers.

BOX 10: Sweating for the Olympics

At factory I, manufacturing sportswear which bears the Olympics emblem, workers (interviewed in October 2003) reported the following conditions:

When there are export deadlines to meet, workers are forced to work shifts as long as 17 hours over six consecutive days.

Workers are exhausted. Many pregnant women suffer miscarriages because of the long working hours.

A quarter of the 2000-strong workforce are employed on temporary contracts. They are paid half the standard monthly wage of permanent workers and are forced to do unpaid overtime when they do not complete their piece-rate targets in the normal working hours.

Union activists are harassed and verbally abused.

Workers, especially temporary workers, are subject to sexual harassment

Workers are verbally abused: *'They call us "dogs" and tell us to go and die.'*

Workers are not receiving any social security pay.

None of the workers knows about labour codes of conduct, nor are they aware of any inspections having taken place.

The Olympics movement can directly influence the sportswear companies by including contractual obligations on labour standards in its licensing and marketing agreements relating to products bearing the Olympics emblem. At the very top of the hierarchy, the IOC is the owner of the rights to all Olympic marks, including the five-ring emblem, and is responsible for the overall direction and management of all Olympics marketing and licensing programmes. While it is the national committees and the organising committees of the Olympic Games themselves that actually issue the licences and marketing contracts, the IOC has the power to determine the overall policies and set the rules. If the movement as a whole made a commitment to respect labour standards, similar to its commitments on protecting the environment, it could play an important role in achieving improvements to working conditions for the many workers who produce sportswear worldwide.

Figure 2: Cause and effect - how the sportswear business model leads to poor working conditions

Executive-level strategies

▶ Outsource production to low-cost locations.

▶ Shorten production cycle.

▶ Minimise production costs to maximise profit.

▶ Minimise inventory costs by shifting packing, warehousing, and freighting to supplier.

▶ Shift forecasting risks to supplier.

....lead to...

Aggressive buying practices

▶ 'Graze' for lowest-cost suppliers.

▶ Push for factories to manufacture products in shorter time.

▶ Push down the price paid to the factory.

▶ 'Just-in-time' production, i.e. place smaller orders more frequently to minimise inventory costs and reduce forecasting risks.

▶ Demand flexibility from the factory managers.

▶ Make supplier pay for faulty orders.

....lead to...

Exploitative management

► Hire workers who are exploitable, low-cost, and easily hired and fired without financial or legal implications.

► Lengthen the working day to meet export deadlines

► Pay by piece rather than time, to reduce costs.

► Set excessive piece-rate targets to force completion of orders in time for export at low cost.

► Refuse to pay minimum wages when orders are low.

► Penalise workers for faulty production, to shift responsibility for quality control.

► Stop workers from joining or forming trade unions

....lead to...

Harsh working conditions

► Excessive working hours and forced overtime.

► Poverty wages and inadequate benefits e.g. sick leave, maternity leave.

► No job or wage security, especially during 'low' season.

► No freedom of association or collective bargaining.

► Poor health.

► Harassment, physical, psychological, and sexual abuse.

► Discrimination.

► Dysfunctional family life.

....the bottom line.

ASICS Corporation: based in Japan, this company is the fifth-largest brand in the global sports-shoe sector. Its motto – 'Bringing up sound youth through sports' – was the inspiration of founder Kihachiro Onitsuka, who was moved to set up his company after witnessing the desperate plight of children in post-war Japan. ASICS is famous for its high-tech running shoes, and its brand has become synonymous with the marathon. In 2002, its global sales amounted to US$ 969 million, with pre-tax profits of US$ 22 million. Sponsoring a number of high-profile Olympic competitors, including marathon runner Naoko Takahashi and popular US high-jumper Amy Acuff, ASICS will expect increased sales throughout this Olympics year. Manufacturing of its products has gradually shifted from Japan to other parts of Asia. ASICS claims that it operates on a principle of *'uniting to achieve goals in the spirit of freedom, fairness, respect for the dignity of the individual and good governance upholding ethical standards while continuing to build corporate value'.* On paper ASICS makes rhetorical reference to its ethical commitments on labour standards, but their practical implementation is insufficient. This report contains evidence of poor practice in an Indonesian factory producing ASICS goods, where workers face excessive overtime, penalties for unmet production targets, sexual harassment by management, and health problems caused by inhaling fabric debris.

Fila: a high-fashion sportswear company of Italian origin, owned since July 2003 by US-based private financier, Sport Brand International, Fila continues to be a household name, particularly among younger consumers. Looking to re-launch its brand in a bid to regain its former financial dominance, the company is investing heavily in advertisements featuring sports and music celebrities, to build its image as a brand of choice. With a marketing budget in excess of US$ 70 million, it has engaged tennis stars like Jennifer Capriati and Kim Clijsters as well as long-distance runner, Adam Goucher. Most of Fila's production takes place in East Asia, and its new supply-chain management strategy aims to reduce delivery lead-times. Fila has made impressive statements of its commitment to respect workers' rights in its supply-chain, but interviews with workers reveal a very different story. Evidence from factories producing for Fila includes reports of excessive working hours, fines for flawed production, intimidation by management for participation in trade-union activities, and workers at risk of dismissal for refusing to do overtime.

Mizuno: Japan's biggest manufacturer of sporting goods and official supplier of uniforms for the International Olympics Committee, Mizuno prides itself on its close affiliation with the Olympics movement. Although smaller in size than some of its competitors, the company has gained accolades for the 'wave' technology used in its running shoes. Some production of its goods still takes place in Japan, but it is moving towards outsourcing in other parts of Asia. The company's strong commitments to environmental protection are championed by its CEO, Masato Mizuno. Unfortunately, its commitments on labour standards are not nearly so strong. At one Chinese factory supplying Mizuno, workers reported working up to eight hours of overtime and having no days off during the peak season, having no basic wage protection during the low season, being fined for flawed products, and being paid piece-rates that vary according to how much work the management wants them to do.

Puma: a German-based athletic apparel and footwear brand, Puma has beaten records on profit growth to become the world's sixth-largest sportswear company. Fast becoming a model in the industry for its successful combination of fashion with performance, this company is snapping at the heels of Nike, Reebok, and Adidas. In 2003, Puma reported doubling its annual profits from US$ 150 million to US$ 320 million. Its three World Cat sourcing organisations place orders directly with suppliers. Ninety per cent of its footwear and 60 per cent of its apparel is sourced from China, Thailand, Malaysia, Vietnam, and Cambodia; further production is based in Romania, Bulgaria, Turkey, Portugal, Italy, Paraguay, and the USA. On labour standards, Puma has taken some promising steps to meet its ethical commitments. A dedicated team of staff check and approve new suppliers and inspect current ones. Puma has initiated worker-education programmes with local organisations. It joined the Fair Labour Association in January 2004. Puma's emphasis on shorter lead times, lower costs, and greater flexibility to increase profits has, however, exacted a heavy toll on the workers in its supply-chain, as evidence in this report shows. Often, its own buying practices have undermined compliance with its code of conduct. As Puma pursues its plan to maintain double-digit sales growth through 2006, it needs to engage in critical self-scrutiny, in order to ensure that *'its published standards are not just hot air'* (Sustainability Report 2003).

Figure 3: Business practices of global sportswear firm

Lotto: founded in 1973 as a local tennis-shoe company, Lotto has grown into a global corporation, selling its tennis shoes and athletic and football apparel and shoes in 70 countries. Owned by Italy Sport Design, its global sales in 2002 amounted to US$ 277.9 million, with profits of US$ 6.4 million. Lotto remains a big name in the tennis world, sponsoring more than 100 tennis players, including Boris Becker, Martina Navratilova, and Thomas Muster. To that, it has added a specialisation in football, sponsoring world-class teams such as the Dutch national soccer team, AC Milan, and Juventus. Lotto outsources all of its production, with suppliers based in Indonesia, Viet Nam, China, Cambodia, the Philippines, and Turkey. In supplier factories surveyed in three countries, workers reported wages below subsistence level; wage cuts and penalties when sick leave is taken; verbal and physical abuse; workers prevented from undertaking trade-union activities; and temporary workers being given excessive production targets and no payment for overtime work. With this kind of exploitation taking place in its supply-chain, Lotto needs to take active measures to implement a strategy to demonstrate that these types of abuse will not be tolerated in the production of Lotto-branded goods.

Kappa: Kappa manufactures, markets, and sells a wide range of athletic apparel and footwear for sport and leisure purposes. In 1994, the company was consolidated into the BasicNet Group. Based in Turin, Italy, the BasicNet Group controls marketing, research and development, finance, and IT services from its headquarters, while conducting its sourcing through the LF Basic Group, a joint venture with Li & Fung, a Hong-Kong based trading company. Distribution is handled through 38 licensees, covering 83 countries. Kappa has captured a large share of the global sportswear market, reporting revenues of US$ 144,473,000 and pre-tax profits of US$ 7,568,000 in 2002. Kappa has invested heavily in sponsorship of sport, especially football. Both the Italian and the Welsh national football teams are Kappa-sponsored. Through the LF Basic Group, Kappa's production is completely outsourced to suppliers in a number of countries, including Taiwan, India, Thailand, China, Viet Nam, Indonesia, Mauritius, Turkey, and Romania. The LF Basic Group is responsible for implementing a Compliance Programme for the Code of Conduct. The code states that all workers should be familiar with the code. If violations are found, inspections of suppliers' facilities are to be conducted in accordance with the code, and the code requires corrective action to be undertaken; but evidence gathered for this report points to the existence of exploitative working conditions in Chinese and Turkish workplaces producing for Kappa, including threats of dismissal for trade-union activities; compulsory overtime, exceeding eight hours over the normal working day in the peak season; and workers being prevented by management from resigning during the peak season. Workers reported ignorance of the existence of a code of conduct on labour practices. Kappa appears to have invested in developing an elaborate Compliance Programme. It needs, however, to ensure that this is genuinely being implemented and is not being undermined by its purchasing practices.

Umbro: a leader in the football market, UK-based Umbro continues to manufacture, market, and sell a range of products for performance and leisure use. It sponsors some of the world's best players, including the English national football teams and world-class individuals such as Liverpool's Michael Owen. Founded in 1920, the company was bought by equity-fund manager Doughty Hanson & Co. in 1999 for £90 million. It is currently up for sale again, with a price tag of £300 million. No public information is available on its sales and profits, because the company is privately owned. Umbro's products are mostly sourced from China and Vietnam. Targeted by the campaign against the use of child labour in football production in 1997, and by further campaigns against the use of 'sweatshop' labour in its supply-chain, Umbro introduced a Code of Conduct on labour practices into its contractual agreements with its suppliers. The company claims to conduct regular visits to factories to check if the code is being complied with, and claims that it works with its suppliers to ensure that standards are met. A letter from Umbro, dated 30 May 2003, states: *'Umbro takes its responsibilities regarding the manufacture of its products very seriously indeed. We work with manufacturing partners who understand and can deliver both our quality and social responsibility requirements.'* But workers in a number of factories supplying Umbro have not felt the impact of Umbro's good intentions. Our research uncovered evidence of workers frequently being made to work an average of 15 hours a day, seven days a week during the peak season; excessive production targets and compulsory overtime without pay; wages as low as US$5 per month during the low season; penalties for flawed production; and dismissal without severance pay. If Umbro's ethical commitments are to ring true, the company needs to analyse its current policies and practices very seriously. In particular, it needs to consider whether the pressures that it puts on its suppliers to meet its demands on price, delivery, and flexibility are making compliance with its code of conduct on labour practices difficult.

Chapter 3
Time to Play Fair

Sportswear factory, Thailand

3: Time to Play Fair

Abuses of the kind documented in the previous chapters have prompted a public outcry against companies who are guilty of perpetuating the misery of workers at the bottom of the supply-chain. Reacting to the threats to their reputations, a common response by companies has been to adopt codes of conduct covering labour practices within their supply-chains. Typically, a company will place obligations on factory managers to comply with the code's provisions, and to accommodate inspections by their buyers or by external auditors engaged for this purpose. Improvements in working conditions have, however, been very modest. Abuses of workers – particularly the more insidious forms of abuse such as excessive working hours, forced overtime, excessive piece-rate targets, job insecurity as workforces expand and contract to accommodate fluctuating orders, and curbs on the right to organise and bargain collectively – still remain an all too common feature in the supply-chains of major sportswear brands. The research conducted for this report suggests three main explanations for this.

1 There is a huge gap between ethical commitments and purchasing practices

In all the sportswear companies researched for this report, their ethical commitments are not reflected in any significant way in the purchasing practices used by their buyers. A recent World Bank report on corporate social responsibility reaches a similar conclusion, stating: *'The majority of the participants [in the survey] acknowledged that unresolved tension among price, quality and delivery time on the one hand, and CSR requirements on the other, risked undermining the credibility of the business case [for social responsibility].'* [37] As far as buying and merchandising staff are concerned, so long as the staff responsible for the ethical policy in the company have vetted a new supplier and have conducted an inspection, it is business-as-usual for them: that is to say, they can continue to place pressure upon the suppliers to deliver goods speedily and flexibly, to push for a low unit price, to squeeze the suppliers' profit margin where possible, and threaten to relocate, indifferent to the consequences for the workers. As a Sri Lankan supplier to Nike put it: *'I wish that there was a system of compliance the other way around, that is to say: (a) buyers do not relocate orders to other suppliers based on a 5 to 10 cent difference in unit price; and (b) that loyalty should be a two-way process – if we suppliers are compliant and open to meeting labour standards, then we should receive consistent orders.'* As sportswear companies choose to pursue short-term rather than longterm business relationships with suppliers, their much-vaunted ethical commitments towards the sustainable development of the producing countries lack all credibility.

A common problem cited by staff responsible for the company's ethical policies is that designers, buyers, and merchandisers expect suppliers to absorb delays on their part in getting the product to the point where it is ready for manufacturing (or 'order-ready', as it is known in the industry); in addition, they expect the factories to bear the risks of poor forecasting of the demand for a product. The factory manager, in turn, shifts these risks on to the workers by expanding working hours to meet export deadlines and expecting them to deal with last-minute product changes; or sub-contracts production to other workplaces or to home-workers in locations that are hidden from any labour-compliance inspections. When things go wrong – for example, where rushed orders result in faulty products – it is the workers who pay the price, as illustrated in Figure 4.

Consequently, even those suppliers that are committed to improving workplace conditions seem unable to meet the heavy demands of the buyers and at the same time comply with the labour standards set by the code. They have to make compromises somewhere, and the factory managers know that so long as they do not indulge in gross abuses of human rights such as using child labour or forced labour, fulfilling the order according to the requirements of time, cost, and quality is the greater priority. In some cases, the factory managers are told by the buyers' staff that they may derogate from certain provisions in the code: for example, during peak season, the number of working hours may increase beyond the maximum set. The disincentive to meet labour standards is very strong in cases where to do so risks losing the client.

'Further progress will be made by providing more and better education to workers concerning their rights, and strengthening the protection of those rights. This should take place through such means as access to public mechanisms for redress of problems, participation in representative trade unions, dialogue with local civil society organisations and participation in private efforts to implement codes of conduct.'

(World Bank Report: 'Strengthening Implementation of Corporate Social Responsibility in Global Supply Chains', 2003)

Some companies have demonstrated an awareness of this tension between their purchasing practices and compliance with labour standards. When interviewed about the gap between the two, the Social Accountability and Environmental Standards Team at Puma answered unequivocally: *'We have to improve on this.'* [38] Nike is planning to incorporate what it calls a 'balanced scorecard approach', which will place compliance with labour standards on a par with cost, quality, and delivery when making decisions on suppliers, as one means of addressing the problem.[39] At Adidas, the Corporate Responsibility Team are currently engaged in a project that is evaluating the impact of their purchasing practices on working hours in suppliers' factories. Although it is yet to be completed, Frank Henke, the head of the team, said: *'Long working hours are a problem for many of our suppliers, and we realise that our own planning processes add to the time pressures on them. We are reviewing and adjusting the internal process of how we plan and give orders to take that pressure off.'* [40] Those who have recognised the need to improve, however, are in the minority.

As if poverty wages and intensification of work are not enough to contend with, sportswear workers must also fear for their jobs as the multinational buyers scour the world for new low-cost, 'one-stop' manufacturing locations in order to maximise profits for the benefit of their shareholders.

In the absence of commitments to a long-term business relationship with suppliers, the sportswear companies' much-trumpeted commitment to ethical investment in the sustainable development of the countries featured in this report rings hollow indeed.

Figure 4: Double standards in the sportswear industry: The factory manager's dilemma

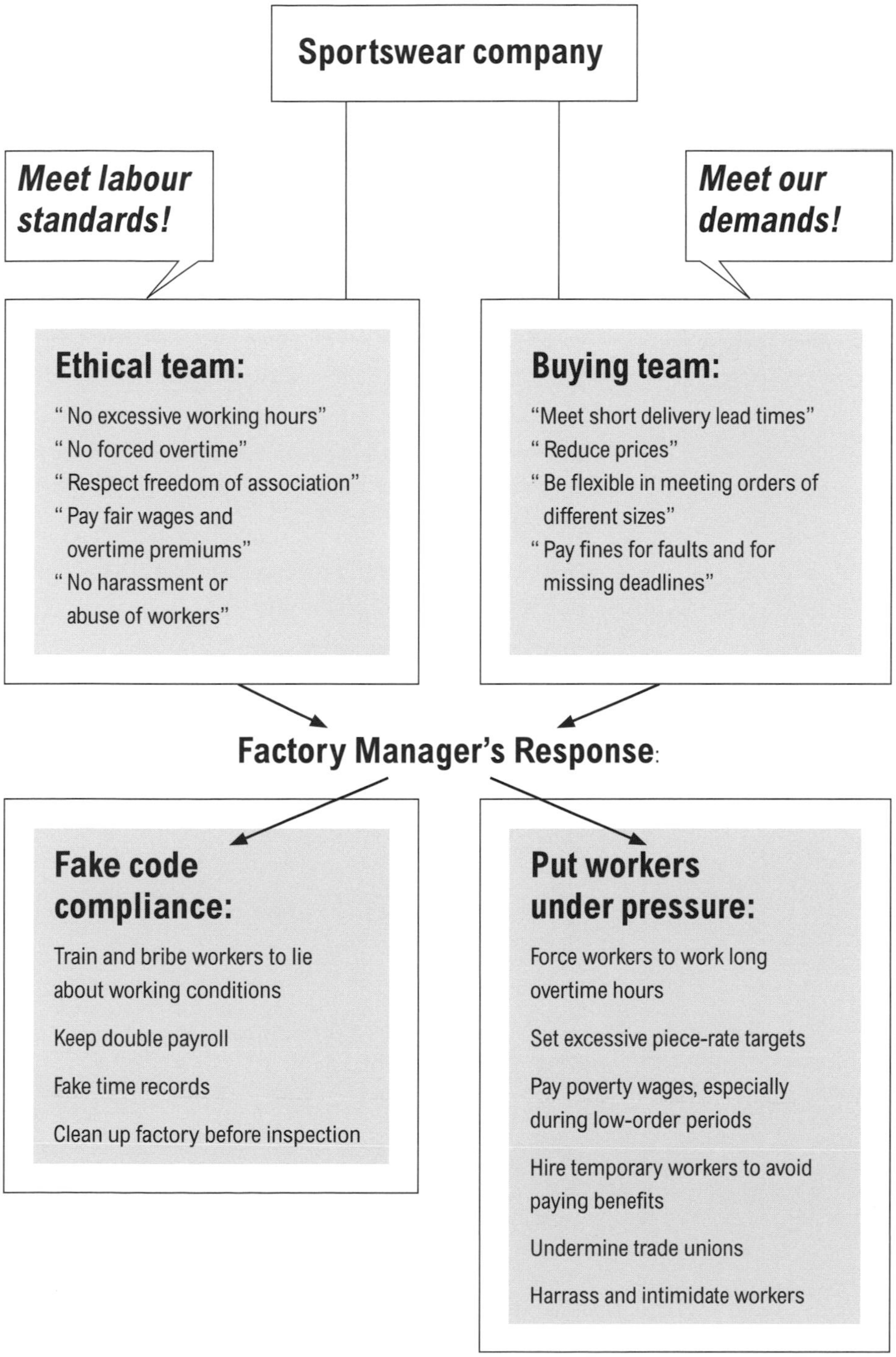

Sportswear company

Meet labour standards!

Meet our demands!

Ethical team:

" No excessive working hours"

" No forced overtime"

" Respect freedom of association"

" Pay fair wages and
    overtime premiums"

" No harassment or
    abuse of workers"

Buying team:

"Meet short delivery lead times"

" Reduce prices"

" Be flexible in meeting orders of
    different sizes"

" Pay fines for faults and for
    missing deadlines"

Factory Manager's Response:

Fake code compliance:

Train and bribe workers to lie
about working conditions

Keep double payroll

Fake time records

Clean up factory before inspection

Put workers under pressure:

Force workers to work long
overtime hours

Set excessive piece-rate targets

Pay poverty wages, especially
during low-order periods

Hire temporary workers to avoid
paying benefits

Undermine trade unions

Harrass and intimidate workers

BOX 11: Breaking the rules

Falsifying the evidence during code-of-conduct inspections is a regular phenomenon in the sportswear industry. This table charts examples cited by workers from five sportswear factories in China.

Factory	Brand	Actual working conditions
R	Adidas, Arena, Fila, Nike, Reebok, Speedo	Wages for piece-rate workers drop below the legal minimum wage to RMB 200-300 (US$ 24-36) per month in the low season. In the peak season, workers routinely work from 7.30 am to 2 am with no day off.
P	Fila, Lacoste, Nike, Reebok, Umbro	The average wage for time-rate workers is between RMB 500 and 600 (US$ 60-72) per month. For those paid on piece-rate, wages often drop to RMB 300-400 (US$ 36-48) during the low season. Fines are imposed for unauthorised leave (three days' wages plus any bonuses) and for flawed production (RMB 50 – US$ 6). Stitching workers regularly work 12-hour shifts. Overtime work during the peak season averages between four and five hours. No premium overtime rate is paid for weekend work
M	Umbro	Piece-rate workers do not receive the legal minimum wage during the low season. During peak season, workers work an average of 15 hours per day, with no day off. Overtime premium is not paid.
N	Mizuno, Kappa	During peak season, workers do between seven and eight overtime hours per day (up to 2 am) and there is no day off. Production-line workers are paid by piece-rate and do not receive wage protection during the low season, when wages fall as low as RMB 300 (US$ 36) per month. The piece-rate payment fluctuates according to the unit price paid by the buyer. Fines of RMB 20-RMB 30 (US$ 2.40-3.60) are imposed monthly for flawed production.

False evidence given during inspection

False payrolls claim that workers receive a guaranteed minimum wage of RMB 345 (US$ 42) per month. The legal minimum in this province is RMB 340 (US$ 41).

Workers are coached to tell auditors that they have minimal overtime and one day off a week.

False wage records state that workers receive between RMB 700 and 800 (US$ 84-96) a month.

No penalties or deductions recorded on false wage records.

Workers are coached to say that they work a maximum of ten hours per day, have two days off per week, and are paid the legal overtime rate.

Workers reported being trained to answer inspectors' questions on 19 topics. Workers who 'perform well' during the inspection are rewarded with RMB 180 (US$ 21.70).

False payrolls state that workers receive a minimum wage of RMB 450 (US$ 54) per month.

Workers are coached to say they work eight regular hours per day and less than three overtime hours per day, and have two days off per week.

The employment contract states that overtime will not exceed three hours per day and that workers are entitled to two rest days per week.

Workers reported being drilled to give the 'right' answers and that the factory was significantly cleaned up in advance of the inspections.

2 The current compliance model is flawed

Despite a general recognition that the most efficient method of implementing and upholding the principles enshrined in codes of conduct is via the recognition of independent trade unions and collective bargaining rights, the sportswear industry is still rife with virulent anti-trade union policies. Sportswear companies and their suppliers demonstrate little more than rhetorical observance of the principles of freedom of association and collective bargaining. Few credible efforts have been made by sportswear companies to counter this trend, either unilaterally within their own supply-chains or at an international level.

Overall, our research suggests that a number of companies are just not serious about their ethical commitments. Superficial and lacking the investment in human and financial resources that are necessary to address the problem seriously, they send out signals of their lack of real concern to their suppliers. Beyond writing the code and sending it to their suppliers for reference, a number of leading sportswear companies seem to be doing little else. In a number of factories supplying sportswear companies that claimed to implement codes of conduct, workers had never even heard of the codes. This was indeed the case at four sportswear factories in Turkey producing for Lotto, Fila, and Kappa. At an Indonesian factory[41] producing for Umbro and Puma, and supplying goods bearing the Olympics emblem, workers interviewed gave emphatic replies: *'There are no codes of conduct on the walls of our factory. We have never read a code of conduct.'*

For a few years now, some more committed companies have been using firms that sell social auditing services to conduct workplace inspections as a means of assessing compliance with labour standards. While these firms' audit teams generally are able to recognise the more visible breaches of labour standards, they tend not to detect the more insidious violations, such as the repression of the right to organise, excessive working hours, or physical, verbal, and sexual harassment of workers. In some instances, to satisfy both the ethical team and the buying team, some factory managers routinely resort to falsifying the evidence when labour-standards inspections are conducted. Workers report that wage records and time records are altered, that they are coached to give the 'right' answers on wages and overtime work, that the factory is cleaned up before an inspection, and that in some cases part of the workforce is put on leave during the inspection days, in order to make the factory appear more spacious.

The 'checklist approach' used by social audit firms is useful in identifying some problems in the workplace. But it fails to identify the *causes* of these problems or suggest effective solutions to overcome them. Conducted in isolation, with little consultation with local stakeholders such as trade unions or women workers' organisations (which have a much better understanding of the workers' situation and of how the local industry operates), these types of social audit are not proving to be the answer to improving working conditions. Further, the failure of these teams to gain the trust of workers, the trade unions, and other credible organisations is a major stumbling block.

Perhaps the biggest flaw in the current compliance model is the fact that workers – who are the main subject of these inspections and audits – are at the edges rather than the centre of the whole system. In some workplaces, even though the code was displayed on the wall of the factory, workers said that they had never been asked about conditions in the workplace, nor had they a clear idea of how it related to their working lives. At one sportswear factory,[42] a worker told researchers: '*Yes, there are codes of conduct pasted on the walls, but they are both in English. They are pasted high up on the wall. It used to be that these codes would only get pasted up when the buyer was around, but since August 2002 they have been up every day. I have read a little bit of the code, but I don't understand much of it.*' With little or no training on their rights as employees, to such workers these codes make no sense, nor do they serve as a useful tool for demanding that their employers accord them their rights. Furthermore, workers' only opportunity to raise their concerns with the brands – and even this is limited through fear of being sacked or by not being picked for interview – is during the infrequently conducted inspections or audits. All in all, this is a system that is not working effectively to bring about significant improvements in working conditions.

3 Bad practices by one company undermine good practices of another

Where different brands are supplied by the same factory, any potential improvements that could be made by one brand's genuine commitments are undermined by the irresponsible behaviour of others. The industry is structured in such a way that most companies share the same suppliers. It is rare to see one brand accounting for more than 70 per cent of the production at a factory. So companies that have made ethical commitments may well be sharing a factory with many other companies which are indifferent to poor working conditions in their supply-chains. Where a given brand is only one of the many customers of a supplier, its ability to encourage observance of labour standards is weakened, since the supplier is more likely to prioritise the demands of other customers with regard to price, delivery times, and flexibility. Our research suggests that, where this is the case, general working conditions remain bad. Where there have been successful resolutions of workers' rights violations, they have tended to result from companies working together and in collaboration with trade unions and NGOs. Some companies, such as Nike, Reebok, Adidas, and Puma, have begun to collaborate with each other, as well as with other companies through multi-stakeholder initiatives. While we see this as an important step forward, we suggest that progress will be limited, unless the sportswear sector as a whole develops a programme of work that promotes trade-union rights, overcomes the limits of the current code-implementation model, and ensures on-going dialogue between the main companies in the sector and the International Textile, Garment and Leather Workers Federation (ITGLWF) via a sectoral or company-wide framework agreement.

Make the change

Sustained campaigning has led some major companies in the sportswear sector to begin to address the appalling working conditions in their supply-chains. Some of these companies have even started to work with NGOs and trade unions to find ways of giving real effect to their ethical commitments. But the scale of their efforts to date is far too small: examples of good practice are sporadic and are concentrated in a few leading companies.

If **sportswear companies** are to be sure that workers' rights are genuinely respected within the supply-chains, they need to do the following:

1) **Develop and implement a credible labour-practices policy.** This should call for suppliers and their sub-contractors to respect internationally recognised labour standards, including all those identified by the ILO as being fundamental rights at work. It should include the right to a living wage, based on a regular working week that does not exceed 48 hours; humane working hours with no forced overtime; a safe and healthy workplace free from harassment; and a recognised employment relationship, with labour and social protection. Some companies have already taken this first step; others clearly have not.

2) **Change their purchasing practices so that they do not lead to worker exploitation.** Companies must take credible and identifiable steps as follows:

▶ Integrate labour-practice policies with current purchasing practices, to prevent the latter from undermining the factories' ability to meet labour standards. This existing tension should be resolved in an integrated way with the factory, buyers, and merchandisers and those responsible for the ethical policy of the company.

▶ Ensure that labour standards are a key criterion when selecting suppliers – alongside indicators of price, time, and quality. Current suppliers should continue to be given support in ensuring that conditions improve in their workplaces.

▶ Stop demanding unrealistic delivery lead-times from suppliers where they result in abusive and exploitative conditions for workers.

▶ Prevent inefficiencies at the company's end of the production cycle being unfairly imposed on the factory. Where delays at the company's end create costs for the factory, allowance should be made for them.

▶ Negotiate a fair price with the supplier: one that reflects the true labour costs of production and allows the supplier to meet ethical labour standards, including fair working hours, payment of a living wage, provision of stable employment contracts, payment of social security, and provision of a healthy and safe working environment.

▶ Develop more stable long-term relationships with suppliers and factories, enabling the latter, in turn, to engage more stable workforces on fairer terms.

▶ Ensure that buyers and merchandisers understand that they are responsible for ensuring that their price, time, and flexibility demands on factories do not undermine labour standards in the workplace.

▶ Ensure that staff responsible for the ethical policy of the company have the mandate to address unethical purchasing practices on the part of the buyers and merchandisers effectively.

3) Implement labour codes of conduct in ways that bring sustainable improvements in working conditions. Companies need to pay particular attention to the following reforms:

▶ Communicate in clear terms to suppliers, factory managers, and their sub-contractors that workers' rights to form and join trade unions and engage in collective bargaining are fundamental to the process of meeting labour standards, and that it is unacceptable to undermine these democratic rights.

▶ Conduct workplace inspections in conjunction with workers, trade unions, and credible local organisations, and ensure that such inspections address all forms of abuse, including insidious abuses such as prevention of trade-union activities, excessive working hours, forced overtime and non-payment of overtime work, poverty wages, unfair piece-rate targets, lack of wage security especially during low seasons, exploitative terms of employment for temporary workers, and non-payment of health and maternity benefits.

▶ Provide accessible and safe means by which workers can report exploitation and abuse and be assured of action on the part of the company; and increase worker training and education programmes, conducted in collaboration with trade unions and credible local organisations, to ensure that workers can use these mechanisms and understand their rights.

▶ Ensure that workers have access to information on what actions have been taken to improve working conditions in their workplace as a result of an inspection or social audit; enable them to report whether these corrective actions have been taken.

4) Work together to address endemic problems in the sportswear industry.
Companies in this sector should take the following steps:

▶ Publicly acknowledge the value of a sector-wide approach to addressing the problems outlined in this report.

▶ Join with trade unions and other concerned organisations in assessing the impacts of the practices of sportswear industry on labour standards; identifying those business strategies and operations which are causing violations of workers' rights; and taking action to address them, giving particular attention to the need to match ethical commitments with actual purchasing practices.

► Join together with trade unions and other concerned organisations in a programme of work which promotes the right of workers to join and form trade unions, which overcomes the limits of the current compliance model, and ensures an ongoing dialogue between the main companies in the sector via a sectoral framework agreement with the International Textile, Garment and Leather Workers Federation. Such an agreement should be aimed at ending the systematic exploitation of workers found within the sector and should be effective in rationalising the existing mechanisms for improving working conditions for sportswear workers.

5) **Inform the public about the working conditions in which their products are made, and provide transparent information about how their business operations affect working conditions in their supply-chains.** Companies should take the following measures:

► Make public information obtained about labour practices in their supply-chains, including information gathered from inspections and social audits.

► Report cases where actions taken to improve working conditions have been agreed with suppliers, and report whether these corrective actions were taken.

Sportswear suppliers and factory managers must accept their direct responsibility to respect their workers' rights. In their bid to take a share of the profits, they must not renege on their responsibilities by breaking labour laws and exploiting or abusing their workers – no matter how competitive the market is. The short-term advantages gained from this type of behaviour are lost in the long term as workers leave the factory or become less productive, de-skilled, unmotivated, and unhealthy. Towards this end, factory managers should routinely adopt the following practices:

A labour-rights demonstration in Indonesia

69

- ▶ Provide their workers with terms and conditions of employment that meet international labour standards and national laws (whichever provides the better protection).

- ▶ Respect the rights of workers to join and form trade unions and to bargain collectively.

- ▶ Provide workers with a living wage based on a regular working week that does not exceed 48 hours, humane working hours with no forced overtime, and a safe and healthy workplace free from harassment.

- ▶ Address the interests of women workers in terms of equal opportunities, child-care and family responsibilities, pregnancy and maternity leave, and freedom to participate in trade-union activities.

- ▶ Ensuring that all workers are legally employed and that employers do not avoid their legal obligations through the abuse of temporary or casual workers.

- ▶ Extend employment benefits such as maternity leave, sick leave, annual leave, health insurance, and wage protection to all categories of workers.

- ▶ Develop sustainable management solutions which allow them to be competitive and productive through investing in their workers' skills, motivation, and well-being.

Governments have much to do to meet their obligations towards workers. They should actively ensure that labour legislation, consistent with international labour standards, is enacted, implemented, and enforced. Particular attention should be given to the following:

- ▶ Protecting the rights of workers in the garment and footwear sector. The specific needs of women workers in terms of health and safety, maternity leave, and child-care provisions are frequently neglected. Further, they are often subjected to wage discrimination and job discrimination without redress.

- ▶ Protecting the right to form and join trade unions and to bargain collectively as a fundamental right. As this report shows, this right is often violated directly by employers, and violations are either condoned by government laws and practice or not punished in any way. Failure on the part of many governments to protect this right has significantly weakened workers' ability to defend their interests, leading to the systematic exploitation and abuse that are prevalent in the sportswear sector.

- Extending labour and social protections and benefits to all categories of workers, whether employed on permanent, temporary, or casual contracts, or as home-workers. In an attempt to 'flexibilise' the workforce, too many governments have allowed employers to employ temporary workers on a rolling basis, thus avoiding their obligations to meet legal requirements on minimum wage payments, benefits, and other forms of worker protection.

- Ensure that workers are paid, as a minimum, a living wage: one that is enough to meet the basic needs of the workers and their families and to provide some discretionary income.

- Strengthening national labour inspectorates and workers' complaint mechanisms.

- Promoting respect for workers' rights at the international level, especially through the ILO.

In the run-up to the Olympic Games in Athens 2004 it is hoped that the **Olympics movement** will make a serious commitment to ensure respect for workers' rights by the sportswear industry at this event and at future games. It can demonstrate its commitment through the **International Olympics Committee (IOC), National Olympics Committees (NOCs), and Organising Committees (OCOGs)** by taking these actions:

- Amend the Olympic Charter to include a specific commitment to respect workers' rights.

- Publicly call for an end to the exploitation of workers and the abuse of workers' rights that are involved in the production of sportswear; and put pressure on the industry to take credible steps towards this.

- For the IOC: adopt a policy requiring that, as a contractual condition of all IOC, NOC, and OCOG licensing, sponsorship, and marketing agreements, labour practices and working conditions involved in the production of Olympics-branded products must comply with internationally accepted labour standards, as defined by the ILO.

▶ Commit resources to implementing an ethical labour-practices policy, including the establishment of mechanisms which address instances of exploitation and abuse of workers in the manufacture of products bearing the Olympics emblem; rigorous inspections of conditions, and prompt attention to complaints of abuse should be made a matter of routine.

Members of the public can play a crucial role in placing pressure upon the sportswear industry to reform its policies and practices. Towards this end, they should raise their voices as follows:

▶ Demand that sportswear companies adopt clear commitments to implement international labour standards in their supply-chains, in addition to guaranteeing a living wage based on a regular working week that does not exceed 48 hours, humane working hours with no forced overtime, and a safe and healthy workplace free from harassment.

▶ Demand that companies ensure that their purchasing practices do not undermine those commitments.

▶ Demand that companies are transparent about their policies and practices relevant to labour practices, and about the impacts of these upon employment terms and working conditions in their supply-chains.

Appendix

Respect for trade-union rights – the gap between rhetoric and reality

Country	Legislation on trade unions	Trade-union rights in practice
Bulgaria	Trade-union rights recognised in law.	Trade unionists face harassment and discrimination. Employers resist collective bargaining.
Cambodia	Trade-union rights protected in law. Law allows employers to exclude unions from bargaining.	Trade-union activity limited: most workers know little of trade unions or their rights. Employers are very hostile to unions, notably in the garment sector. Union activists face intimidation and dismissal. In January 2004, union leader Chea Vichea was murdered after receiving death threats reportedly linked to his political and union activities.
China	Trade unions recognised only within official structures. Freedom of association recognised in constitution but not in trade union law. Protection of right to strike was removed from constitution in 1982.	All attempts at establishing workers' organisations outside official structures are repressed, often through imprisonment. Workers, especially migrants, are subject to violations of labour and other human rights. Labour law often flouted.
Indonesia	Right to form trade unions recognised, but within strong limitations. Government interference sanctioned by law.	Much protest and strike action, but usually 'illegal' for failing to follow lengthy mediation procedures. Unionists face employer intimidation and unfair dismissal, protestors face police violence.
Thailand	The law recognises trade-union rights and collective bargaining, and prohibits anti-union discrimination by employers. The right to strike is recognised.	In practice, collective bargaining is not ensured. Only a small proportion of workers are covered by a collective agreement. In December 2003, 269 workers in an apparel factory were arrested for striking illegally. Most of these workers were Burmese migrants with legal working permits.
Turkey	Trade-union rights recognised, but with heavy restrictions, notably on bargaining and the right to strike.	Collective bargaining is often obstructed, there are reports of harassment, union-busting, and strike-breaking. Union leaders have been imprisoned for their activities, and can face ill-treatment in detention.

ICFTU produces an annual survey of trade union rights violations, which can be found at this address: www.icftu.org/survey

Background research reports

APLU (2003) 'Interviews with Taiwanese suppliers to sportswear companies', Taipei: Oxfam GB

BEPA (2003) 'Puma in Bulgaria', Clean Clothes Campaign

Cunliffe, L. (2003) 'The Garment Sector Business Model for Purchasing Practices throughout the Supply-chain', Oxford : Oxfam GB

Kaya, E. S. (2003) 'Sportswear Factories in Turkey', Ankara: Clean Clothes Campaign

Muchlala, B. and T. Connor (2003) 'Working Conditions in Indonesian Sportswear Factories in Jakarta and Bandung EPZ Areas', Jakarta : Oxfam GB and Oxfam Community Aid Abroad

Womyn's Agenda for Change (2003) 'Fashion and its Victims', Phnom Penh: Oxfam GB

Womyn's Agenda for Change (2003) 'Interviews with Workers on Working Conditions in the Cambodian Sportswear Sector', Phnom Penh: Oxfam GB

Yimprasert, J. and Thai Labour Campaign (2003) 'Supply Chains in the Thai Garment Industry: the Impact on Workers', Bangkok: Oxfam GB

Notes

[1] This includes the International Confederation of Free Trade Unions (ICFTU), the ten Global Union Federations (GUFs), and the Trade Union Advisory Committee (TUAC) to the OECD. The GUFs consist of the International Textile, Garment and Leather Workers Federation (ITGLWF) representing the textile-sector unions, as well as Education International, International Confederation of Free Trade Unions, International Federation of Building and Wood Workers, International Federation of Chemical, Energy, Mine and General Workers' Union, International Federation of Journalists, International Metalworkers' Federation, International Transport Workers' Federation, International Union of Food, Agricultural, Hotel, Restaurant, Catering, Tobacco and Allied Workers' Association, Public Services International Trade Union Advisory Committee to the OECD, Union Network International.

[2] Mamic (2003) 'Business and Code of Conduct Implementation: How firms use management systems for social performance' (International Labour Organisation).

[3] Amounts converted from Baht to US$.

[4] Factory L and Factory M.

[5] Factories W, X, Y, and Z.

[6] Factory CA.

[7] Factory L and Factory M.

[8] Factory N.

[9] Factory W.

[10] Factory CD.

[11] With the permission of workers, the Clean Clothes Campaign alerted Lotto to research indicating examples of abusive working conditions in this factory. Lotto responded by placing pressure upon its UK licensee, which directly manages the relationship with the factory, to address the situation. It is likely that an audit of this factory will take place this year.

[12] Factory V.

[13] Factory CE.

[14] Factory H.

[15] 'Sporting Goods Industry Market Facts', Athletic Footwear and Apparel 2003.

[16] 'US sporting goods imports resume growth', 6 March 2003, SGMA press release.

[17] With shoe production, sports-brands are generally choosing to build long-term relationships with a few suppliers, often choosing to deal directly with the manufacturer rather than through an agent or supply-chain manager. Conversely, with apparel, companies will 'graze' among a wide variety of suppliers, placing smaller orders with a larger number of manufacturers. See Mamic (2003) op. cit.

[18] This is particularly true for apparel. See footnote 17 and also NOVIB-commissioned study by I. Zeldenrust and N. Ascoly: 'East and Southeast Asia Regional Labour Research Report', August 2003.

[19] Clean Clothes Campaign (forthcoming, March 2004), 'Report on Small Sports Brands'.

[20] ACONA, 'Managing Your Supply-chain: A Choice Between Ethics and Competitive Advantage?', February 2004.

[21] See also N. Ascoly, 'Pricing in the Global Garment Industry', Report from an international seminar organised by IRENE, Clean Clothes Campaign, and EED, held on 20 February 2003 at Mulheim an der Ruhr, Germany.

[22] P. Changsorn, 'Regional hub – Nike see potential in Thailand', *The Nation*, 29 September 2003.

[23] Email correspondence with Mr Reiner Seiz, General Manager, global sourcing and logistics, 28 November 2003.

[24] Interview with factory owner, October 2003.

[25] Interview with owner of factory EC, December 2003.

[26] Nike did eventually return to the Sri Lankan supplier – and agreed to the higher price – because it made a better-quality product.

[27] Factory C and E

[28] Factory U.

[29] Factory I.

[30] Factory Q.

[31] Factory M.

[32] Factory L.

[33] This company is also an official licensee for Nike, Reebok, Manchester United, and Diadora. It is also a licensed manufacturer for Puma in Australia.

34 Factory D.

35 Interview by Oxfam, 6 August 2003.

36 Recent developments may signal a change of heart by the World Bank. In January 2004, the World Bank's private-sector lending arm, the International Finance Corporation (IFC), extended a loan to Grupo M, a large Dominican Republic garment manufacturer, to set up facilities in Haiti. During the loan negotiations, trade unions released video testimony of violence instigated by Grupo M against workers seeking to form trade unions. As a result, the loan was only approved on the condition that the company explicitly recognised its employees' rights to freedom of association and collective bargaining. The IFC is now considering including core labour standards as a statutory loan requirement in all its lending.

37 H. Jorgensen, M. Pruzan-Jorgensen, M. Jungk, and A. Cramer (2003) 'Strengthening Implementation of Corporate Social Responsibility in Global Supply Chains' (World Bank Group). A recent ILO report reaches a similar conclusion, stating that 'The fundamental challenge that exists across sectors is the need to integrate CSR into sourcing, something which is occurring at a slow pace, if at all.' See Mamic (2003) op. cit.

38 Interview by Oxfam, 6 August 2003.

39 Email correspondence with Maria Eitel, Vice-President for Corporate Social Responsibility at Nike, 6 February 2004

40 Interview by Oxfam, 6 August 2003.

41 Factory I.

42 Factory H.

The Clean Clothes Campaign (CCC) is an international coalition of consumer organizations, trade unions, researchers, human rights groups, solidarity activists, migrant, homeworker and women workers' organizations, Fair Trade Shops and many other organizations, which aims to improve working conditions in the global garment industry. The Clean Clothes Campaign is based in 11 European countries, has approximately 250 member organizations and works closely with partner organizations in many garment-producing countries. **http://www.cleanclothes.org**

Oxfam is a rights-based confederation of affiliated organizations working in more than 100 countries to find lasting solutions to poverty and injustice. Oxfam affiliates are working together with others to build a global movement of citizens campaigning for economic and social rights. Oxfam believes that economic growth must be balanced with social equity to achieve a just and sustainable world.

Oxfam affiliates participating in the Play Fair at the Olympics Campaign are Oxfam America, Oxfam-in-Belgium, Oxfam Canada, Oxfam Community Aid Abroad (Australia), Oxfam GB, Intermón Oxfam (Spain), Oxfam Ireland, Novib Oxfam Netherlands, Oxfam New Zealand, Oxfam Quebec and Oxfam Germany. See **www.maketradefair.com** and **www.oxfaminternational.org**

Global Unions: the name "Global Unions" is used for the major institutions of the international trade union movement. Global Unions comprises:

▶ the International Confederation of Free Trade Unions (ICFTU), which represents most national trade union centres. Most individual unions relate through their national union centre to the ICFTU which has 233 affiliated organisations in 152 countries and territories on all five continents, with a membership of 151 million.

▶ the ten Global Union Federations (GUFs),the international representatives of unions organising in specific industry sectors or occupational groups (EI, ICEM, IFJ, ITGLWF, PSI, ITF, IFBWW, IMF, IUF, & UNI - for full names, see **www.global-unions.org**).

▶ the Trade Union Advisory Committee to the OECD (TUAC)

An individual union will usually belong to a national union centre in its country, which will then affiliate to a world body such as the ICFTU. The same individual union will also usually affiliate to a GUF relevant to the industry where it has members. The ICFTU and ITGLWF (International Textile, Garment and Leather Workers' Federation) are the Global Unions organisations most closely involved with the campaign at the international level.

Photo: CCC

In August 2004 the world's athletes will gather in Athens for the Summer Olympic Games. Global sportswear firms will spend vast sums of money to associate their products with the Olympian ideal. Images of Olympic events, complete with corporate branding, will be televised to a global audience.

The expansion of international trade in sportswear goods under the auspices of corporate giants such as Nike, Adidas, Reebok, Puma, Fila, ASICS, Mizuno, Lotto, Kappa, and Umbro has drawn millions of people, mainly women, into employment. From China and Indonesia to Turkey and Bulgaria, they work long hours for low wages in arduous conditions, often without the most basic employment protection. The rights to join and form trade unions and to engage in collective bargaining are systematically violated.

This report asks fundamental questions about the global sportswear industry – questions that go to the heart of debates on poverty, workers' rights, trade, and globalisation. *'Olympism'*, in the words of the Olympic Charter, *'seeks to create a way of life based on … respect for universal fundamental ethical principles.'* This report shows that the business practices of major sportswear companies violate both the spirit and the letter of the Charter. Yet the Olympics movement, particularly the International Olympics Committee, has been remarkably silent in the face of these contraventions.

During this Olympic year when such a high value is put on fair play, we ask you to join workers and consumers world wide who are calling for change across the whole of the sportswear industry. You can ask the International Olympics Committee and all sportswear companies to take action now. Log on to **www.fairolympics.org**

www.fairolympics.org

ISBN 0-85598-535-6

9 780855 985356 >

PLAY FAIR
AT THE OLYMPICS

Oxfam

MAKE
TRADE
FAIR

Clean Clothes Campaign

GLOBAL UNIONS